TEACHING OF HISTORY

NIRMAL YADAV

ANMOL PUBLICATIONS PVT. LTD.
NEW DELHI - 110 002 (INDIA)

ANMOL PUBLICATIONS PVT. LTD.
H.O.: 4374/4B, Ansari Road, Darya Ganj,
New Delhi-110 002 (India)
Ph.: 23278000, 23261597
B.O.: No. 1015, Ist Main Road, BSK IIIrd Stage
IIIrd Phase, IIIrd Block
Bangalore - 560 085 (India)
Visit us at: www.anmolpublications.com

Teaching of History

First Edition, 1994

Reprint, 1996, 1998, 1999, 2000, 2001, 2003, 2004, 2005

Reprint, 2006
Reprint, 2008

PRINTED IN INDIA

Printed at Mehra Offset Press, Delhi.

Preface

This book has been written to meet the requirements of pupil-teachers in colleges of education and participating teachers working in our schools. The book has been written in a systematic way using a simple language and explaining all details to make it easily understandable. It is likely to help the teachers to develop in their students various qualities such as those of national integration, international understanding, cooperation, tolerance etc.

The book broadly covers the B.Ed. syllabus of various Indian universities and is uptodate in all respects. Suggestions for the further improvement of the book shall be thankfully accepted.

Author

Contents

Chapter 1

Meaning and Scope of History

1.1 INTRODUCTION

In a democratic country like our a common educational programme is not only desirable but quite essential. It is our sacred duty to chalk out such an educational programme for our masses that may develop in them the qualities of good citizenship, loyalty to democracy and civic responsibility. It should also enkindle in them such moral and spiritual values that ultimately give meaning to life. These are the broader objectives of our national education policy. To attain some of these objectives, the teaching of history plays an important role. It acquaints the future citizens of the country of their past and prepares such a background in their conception on the basis of which they may build up their present and prepare for future.

History deals with our social, political and economical aspects of life. Though History is an independent subject in many an Indian states but in some states it is taught as a past of social studies. No doubt, History dominates the entire course of social studies and forms its major and important part.

1.2 WHAT IS HISTORY ?

The word "History" has been derived from the greek word "Historia" which means "what has actually happened in the past". Thus history is just "man—his story."

History is an important subject because it tells us about the human civilisation of the past days. In the words of a famous historian, history is, "what men have done and said and above all what they have thought." According to Johnson, "History has always been what human beings thought about the past and in this sense it has always been of creation of the past."

From the mass of details, available about man's recorded past it can easily been seen that history is the story of man's effort to satisfy his craving for an orderly social life, to satisfy his love for freedom and to satisfy his thirst for beauty and knowledge.

To under the wide divergence about the measuring of history let us give here a few definitions of history.

In the words of Henary Johnson,[1] "history is a detailed account of the events that have taken place". From this definition it became quite clear that history mainly deals with the events of the past. In history there is description of the events only.

"History is the record of man's steps and slips. It shows us that the steps have been slow and slight: the slips, quick and abounding. It provides us with the opportunity to profit by the stumbles and tumbles of our fore-runners. Viewed a right, History is the broadest studies, embracing every aspect of human life. It lays the foundation of education by showing how mankind repeats it errors and what those errors are. Bismarck used to remark, "fools say that they learn by experience. I prefer to learn by other people's experiences." These study of history offers us that opportunity. It is universal experience—infinitely longer, wider and more varied than any individual's experience."[2]

Dr. Radhakrishnan has defined history as, "The memory of a nation or a race."

In view of some historians it is a "new date calendar" while others consider it a "collection of events of war."

The definition given by *Rapson* is quite scientific. According to him, "History is a Connected account of the course of events and the progress of ideas".

In the words of Prof. Ghose, "history is a scientific study and record of our complete past".

Tagore says, "There is only one history—The History of Man." In the words of Pt. Jawahar Lal Nehru, "History is the story of Man's struggle through the ages against Nature and the elements; against wild beasts and the jungle and some of his own kind who have tried to keep

1. Henry Johnson, *Teaching of History*, p. 1.

2. B. M. Laddell Hart, *Why does not we learn from History*, p. 2.

him down and to exploit him for their own benefit".

"History is the record of what one age finds worthy to note in another," remarks Burckhardt.

Jones Opines says, "History is a veritable mine of life experiences and the youth of today studies History that he may profit by the experiences of the race".

In *Carr's* words, "History is a continuous process of interaction between the historian and his facts. It is an unending dialogue between the present and the past".

Keeping in view all these interpretations regarding the nature and concept of History, we may say that History is not a mere chronicle of events as generally understood by common man. It is actually, "a wrath, with the events strung on the thread of the ideas".

"History is not simple information regarding the affairs of kings also have passed away but is a science which expands the intellect and furnishes the wise with examples."[3]

In the end it would suffice to say that history deals with all the worldly affairs pertaining to human beings.

1.3 HISTORICAL DEVELOPMENT OF HISTORY

Here we include a brief account of development of history to show how immensely it has grown in depth and notion.

Wrong Notion About History

In view of the remarks made by **Napolean** that, "history is a fable agreed upon", people started thinking that they cannot consider history to the quite dependable thing and actually it is not quite dependable.

Spencer has remarked, "Read them (the facts of history) if you like, for amusement, but do not flatter yourself. They are instructions".

In view of some thinkers, "God manifested himself in history".

In the opinion of **Freud,** "Historical records are a law of right or wrong".

3. *Tarikh-e-Daudi.*

According to **Jones**, "History is a precious store-house of the experiences of human race. History is recorded so that people may take advantage of the experience of people of the past generation".

Henry Johnson opines, "History is itself a phase of development and, therefore, never entirely new. History began as enquiry and is still enquiry. History began as a record and is still a record. History became what actually happened and is what actually happened".

Old Concept of History

From the foregoing discussion it becomes evident that in the older days and upto the mediaeval times, history dealt with kings and queens, their ministry and courtiers, their generals and warriors and sometimes national heroes.

In the beginning history was nothing more than a local saga, a collection of legendary stories, heroic ballads and folk-tales, sung in praise of great heroes on ceremonial occasions. Its aim was partly to provide entertainment and partly to breathe heroism into the hearts of young warriors on the eve of some battle. In these histories facts and fictions were quite freely mixed up together.

The credit of giving history the status of an independent field of study goes to the Greek historian **Herodotus**, who lived in 5th century B.C. He collected a lot of information about present and past of places and then gave an interesting narration of these.

Thucydides, a contemporary of **Herodotus** gave a true picture of political conditions and events of his own time and not of past. His writings can be called "didactic history" and in his field he still remains a model and master. For the next two thousand years history remained either story-telling history or didactic history.

Change in Concept

In the 19th century with the advance of physical sciences, attitudes of the students of history completely changed. Germany became the house of scientific history. The history was raised to the level of a science, during this period by two great German historians (i.e. Leopold Von Ranke and Nietruhr). They used scientific principles and methods. Because of such a vast change in attitude the 19th century in called "the century of history". However, it may be clearly noted that this age being the age of empires, monarchies and political alignments, history emphasised mainly the military and political aspects of human life. It was not at a later date under the influence of Karl Marx that emphasis was shifted from political to economic and social aspects of man and cultural history came to be recognised as an invaluable aspect of the achievements of mankind.

Concept of Indian History

History in India has an oral tradition. The achievements of ancient Indian heroes were preserved in the form of sagas and gathas. The 'bards' and other people used to learn by heart various events and deeds of the people, because the arts of writing and printing books were unknowns. The historical events were used to literory, artistic, political and religious purposes.

In "puranas" and other historical writings of India, events have not been arranged in a systematic and chronological order. There is more of praise of kings and warriors.

It was only under the English system of education that history was introduced as a school subject in India. Most of the text-books an Indian History were written by European scholar, who have no clear understanding of Indian society and its problems. The result was that history in Indian schools had little educational value, either individual or social.

Modern Concept of History

We can state the modern concept of history as under:

1. *History is a scientific study and a faithful record of our complete past:* According to its modern concept, history is not confined to one period or country or nation. It begins from the appearance of man on this earth and deals with all places whose man has gone and lived. It also deals with various aspects, such as political, social, economic, religious, literary, aesthetic etc., of human life. It has now actually become a study of man's evolution on earth.

2. *History is a study of the present in the light of the past:* The present social life of man has been a result of evolution through centuries of human efforts in various directions. Modern history helps us in understanding the process of evolution and how society has come

to its present form. It also helps us to discover and explain how this adjustment has taken place in the past and how it is taking place today. It is likely to give us not only a sense of national patriotism and an appreciation of national heritage but also a clear sense of world unity and world citizenship.

3. *History is an evolution, growth and development of human civilisation through the ages*: We have seen that history is always on the move and never static. Since it is dynamic so it implies growth, development and evolution. "It traces the fascinating story of how man has developed through the ages, how man has studied to use and control his environment and how the present institutions have grown out of the past. Man's struggle with his environment, man's use and abuse of his powers and resources, his development and essential unity of human civilization are the main themes of history."

1.4 IS HISTORY A SCIENCE OR AN ART ?

There has been a lot of discussion as to whether history is a science or an art?

I. History as a Science

In the opinion of some scholars history is a science. As a science it aims at discovering facts of the past as they really were and then interpreting them correctly. It also makes use of various methods of enquiry like observation, classification, formulation of the hypothesis and analysis of evidence before interpreting and reconstructing the past.

Science has been defined in various ways. According to Galbraith, "By science we mean a body of knowledge that seeks to tell the truth, the whole truth and nothing but the truth."

Science has also been defined as a "*Systematic study of knowledge*" concerning the relationship between cause and effect of a particular phenomenon.

History too, "is an inquiry, designed to find the truth" so it is a science.

Strictly speaking history cannot be termed as science. It is not a science in the sense physics and chemistry are sciences. It is so because history is not based on certain theories and the facts of history are too complicated and unique. They seldom repeat in the real sense of the word. Historical data are not available for observation and experimentation.

It may be called a concrete science because it is concerned with the experiences of human beings.

Sciences are of two kinds, physical science and social science. History is not a physical science but it is certainly a social science. It may not use the methods of physical sciences but it do use the methods of social science in the following form :

(i) in it, we have a collection of data. Such data may be secured from any quarter. The whole of the data that forms history has been collected at a place,

(ii) the collected data can be analysed quite carefully, it can be classified and sorted out. The laboratory of history is the universe, and

(iii) we can lay down certain theories after proper observation, analysis and comparative inspection of the available data.

II. History as an Art

Many scholars consider that history is an art. Art is nothing but the practical application of knowledge acquired by science. Art is also a part of literature and Fine Art. Here we have a display of emotions and fine feelings. This element is also available in history.

In the words of **Spencer**, "History deals with unroganised facts from which no conclusions can be drawn." In addition to this they give the following arguments to show that history is not a science no conclusions can be drawn". Besides this statement, Spencer and his followers have based their arguments on the following facts:

1. *Historical Methods of Arriving at Facts Differ Radically from the Methods of Natural Sciences*: Natural sciences generally deal with facts which can be observed directly and which can be tested by experiment. Historical facts on the other hand, cannot be observed directly. They can be arrived at only indirectly through inference and through various sources. This indirect method of history is plainly a different method and the general status of facts, established by this method, is also quite different.

2. *Historical Synthesis Cannot be Entirely Scientific in the Sense of Natural Sciences*: The fundamental quest in history is for what is

important. As such historical synthesis is completely different from that of natural sciences. In history, past must be seen through the eyes of the past and not through the eyes of the present. If history is determined by what matters most in the present, it would inevitably miss what mattered most in the past and would, therefore, "neither correctly represent nor correctly explain the past." As Walsh says, "The historian is taking not as a scientist would, about all men, past present and future, who have certain characteristics, but about all the man who lived at a certain time and in a certain area.[4]

3. *Historical Data are not Available for Scientific Observation and Experiment*: History deals with thoughts and actions of human beings, who possess a tree will. Collingwood says that every historical event has two aspects, the internal and the external. Its outside describes the external factors and inside, the thoughts and feelings of the people, involved in the event. The historian is concerned with both these aspects because he investigates the actions which depict both the outside and the inside of an event. "Events of history are the things which the historian looks, not at, but through, to discern the thought within.[5] And free human activities cannot provide material for scientific experimentation and formulation of scientific laws. Moreover, experiment in history is not possible because it deals with events that have already happened and cannot be repeated. *Secondly*, the intentions which a human action expresses, cannot be directly observed. These can only be reached by a process of inference and apprehended through the imaginative powers of the mind.

4. *In History, we can Neither Formulate Generations nor Predict the Future with Certainty*: Science consists of a body of general truths. A scientist looks at knowledge from a universal angle and arrives at certain generalizations. This helps him to control the present and predict the future. But for a historian, it is not possible to arrive at general principles or laws which may enable him to predict with certainty the recurrence of like events, under given conditions."

Conclusion

From the above discussion we may conclude that history is an art as well as science. As an enquiry to elicit truth it is science and as a narrative account of that truth it is an art or a piece of literature. Science supplies only day lifeless facts and it is only historian with great literary

4. Walsh—*An Introduction to Philosophy of History*, p. 40.
5. Collingwood—*The Idea of History*, p. 214.

genius, high imagination and sympathetic bent of mind, who puts life and soul into lifeless historical events and thus makes history live for us.

Hence history may be considered as a science and historiography, an art. However, for a historian both these facts (i.e., history and historiography) are important. In history knowledge and action both go together. In the words of Lord Action, "Study of history is critical, objective and view." In this statement he has put in the elements of both science and art.

Presently the historian is expected not only to keep himself abrest of recent trends in historical research and interpretations but he has also to reconstruct the life of the past, re-interpret the process of history and also to represent the historical truths in the light of the latest researches and discoveries, without any bias or falsehood.

1.5 SCOPE OF HISTORY

History is one of the oldest subjects of study. By history we understand the breadth, comprehensiveness, variety and extent of learning experiences, provided by the study of a particular subject. The growth of history has accompanied with the growth of human race. Thus history and man are inter-related or that history is a story of human race from beginning upto the present day. History at present is no more confined to the study of political activities of man but it also includes a study of his achievements in the physical, social, economic, religious, philosophical, literary, artistic, cultural, industrial, technological and scientific fields, starting from ancient times upto the modern age. In this way its scope is very wide and varied—infact as wide as the world and as long as the existence of man on earths. History links the present of mankind with his past. We cannot say that future is outside the scope of history. Experiences of history will form the history of tomorrow and in this way history is connected with future as well.

The most interesting fact about the extent and comprehensiveness of history is that today we hear of "History of Art," "History of Culture," History of Civilization," "History of Religion," "History of Music," "History of Geography," "History of Physics," "History of Philosophy," "History of Education," "History of Biology," "History of the Atom," "History of Literature," "History of Mathematics," and History of what not. A learned speaker on a political, religious, literary or any other platform connected with any field of human activity, will place before his audience pure and simple history, connected with the life and achievements of some past of great human beings and nothing else. This makes the scope of history almost limitless, which knows no ends and also speaks of the importance of history as a teaching subject in schools and colleges.

The wide Scope of History is shown in the following diagram:

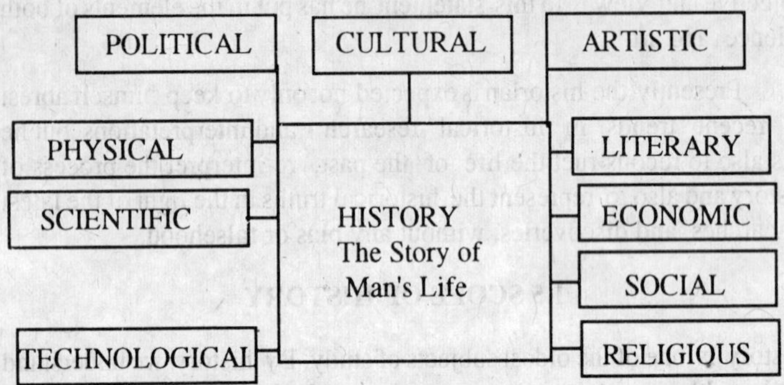

Thus, history has expanded both vertically and horizontally. Its close connection with the allied fields of human sciences, has given new effects to historical studies.

In the words of *Lord Action*, "If the past has been an obstacle and a burden, a knowledge of past is the safest and surest emancipation".

In the words of *E. Lewis Hasluck*, "A knowledge of history illumines the whole of human life. It adds to our knowledge of the existing state of world, a knowledge in which the human society and institution has grown up, a knowledge for future."

From the above discussion at becomes clear that the subject of history has no frontiers and that it is limitless and fathomless ocean, with no ends in view. However for instructional purposes in schools and colleges, we have to limit its scope and frontiers.

For deriving fullest benefit of historical studies, we should place before our students the broad out-lines of development down the ages on one hand and the detailed study of a short period of history, on the other. The former will provide the whole sweep of the story of the past while the latter will give the varied aspects of the life of a people for a chosen period. In this way both the vertical and horizontal aspects of history, will be studied together and provide full benefit to the education of our rising generation.

REVISION QUESTIONS

1. What do you mean by the term: History ? How is it interpreted in its modern context ?
2. History is said to be an all-embracing subject. How far do you agree with this statement and why ?
3. Trace briefly the historical development of the subject of history.
4. What is the modern concept of history ?
5. Is history a science or an art ?
6. Discuss briefly the scope of history.
7. "The scope of history is wide, the theme is the whole life of man, the world over."

   In the light of the above statement, discuss briefly the scope of history.
8. "Inspite of the fact that history is an all-encompassing subject it has its frontiers."

   Elucidate this statement by discussing the nature and scope of history.
9. "History is scientific study and a record of our complete past." (Ghate) Comment and discuss the nature of History as a science.
10. To what extent can you consider History a science ? What utility do you expect to derive from its study in Indian Schools?

Chapter 2

Aims, Objectives and Values of Teaching History

2.1 INTRODUCTION

For the proper teaching of a subject it is essential to have a knowledge of aims and objectives of teaching that subject. It is also true for the teaching of history. In the absence of clear aims and objectives, the teacher will be leading his pupils as a journey without destination.

Unless we determine the aims, it is not possible for us to work out a plan for attaining those aims. Once the aims and objectives are determined, then various methods of teaching are evolved according to these aims and objectives. Formulation of aims also helps in keeping the teacher and taught on the right track. Aims and objectives indicate the way and point to the ideas. No doubt aims are idealistic, but they are indispensable.

Writing in this context Henderson says, "we teachers, need to know where we want to go. Otherwise we may walk a long way, get very tired and accomplish practically nothing".[1]

For determining the aims of teaching any subject we have to take into consideration the utility and usefulness of that subject. We have material as well as spiritual aspects in our life. For a successful spiritual life it is essential that we have a well-founded material life.

The aims and objectives of teaching various subjects are normally very similar and they are generally guided by economic and social consideration. The aims and objectives of teaching history include all the aims and objectives of education. These aims and objectives of teaching history have undergone changes with the change in the

1. Henderson, S.V.P. *Introduction of Philosophy of Education*, 1947, p. 15.

philosophical thinking of the time and changes in social and political practices.[2]

In the nineteenth century the effects of Karl, August, Muller and Von Ranke bore signs of present day aims of teaching history. Towards the close of the century, if one surveyed the different aims of teaching history, one would find the aims frequently mentioned to be accruing from historical instruction were: discipline of the memory, the imagination, the judgement; the setting up of ideas of patriotism, of conduct, of social service; the illumination of other studies especially geography and literature; and the establishment of intimate relations with current events. Apart from these, training in historical evidence; training to develop habits of accuracy in dealing with facts; skill in putting facts together, and insight into causal relations; training in the use of books and the cultivation of a discriminating taste for historical reading were also considered important.[3]

2.2 AIMS AND OBJECTIVES OF HISTORY TEACHING IN INDIA

In our own country we had very few historical texts and writings before the advent of Muslims. "History," as Basham remarks, "in fact, in so far as it existed (in India) was a branch of religion......"[4] Its aim was to instruct the pupils in Dharma (morals), Artha (wealth), Kama (desire) and Moksha (salvation). The Ramayana and the Mahabharata throw a flood of light on the lives of people and the "ideals they were expected up to".

Kalhana was to first to scientifically analyse past events and present them in an artistic way.

Various periods of history such as the Muslim history, European history, history of England and history of India were taught in such a way as to fulfil the requirements of examination and syllabus for these school subjects.

When the Secondary Education Commission formulated the objectives of secondary education as, "the training of character to fit the students to participate creatively as citizens in the emerging social

2.Johnson, Henry, *Teaching of History*, New York Macmillan Company, 1940, p. 25.

3. Johnson, Henry, *Ibid.*, p. 108.

4. Basham, A.L., *The Indian Sub-continent in Historical Perspective*, p. 23.

order, the improvement of their practical and vocational efficiency so that they may play their part in building up the economic prosperity of their country; and the development of their literary, artistic and cultural interests which are necessary for self-expression and for the full development of human personality without which a living national culture cannot come into being."[5] In the light of these aims the social studies movement was given a trial for about a decade. However, now we have again switched over to the old pattern of instructions.

The aim of history, as given in its report by Kothari Commission,[6] is "to increase productivity, achieve social and national integration, accelerate the process of modernisation and cultivate social, moral and spiritual values." The role of history in strengthening "social and national integration" and cultivation of social, moral and spiritual values cannot be minimised.

Aims of Teaching History

In the foregoing discussion we have already given a broad hint to the aims of teaching history. In this sub-section these are listed in a more systematic and easily understandable form.

Though history teaching may not be able to achieve all the aims of education, such as:

(i) development of qualities of ideal citizenship,

(ii) development of qualities of leadership,

(iii) all round development of personality, and

(iv) development of character building and economic efficiency,

yet it is helpful in the achievement of some of these aims, e.g. development of qualities of citizenship, qualities of leadership, character building etc.

As already pointed out the aims of teaching history have changed many a times in the past. They can be classified as:

(i) aims of teaching history in ancient times,

(ii) aims of teaching history in the 19th century, and

(iii) aims of teaching history in modern times.

5. Government of India, *Report of Secondary Education Commission*, 1952-53, p. 23.
6. Government of India, *Report of the Education Commission*, 1966, p. 613.

We shall take up these one by one.

(i) Aims of Teaching of History in Ancient Times : In ancient times history was only a chronology of events. It was intended to preserve the memorable events of life. In those days, history was a part of literature. Then the main aim of teaching of history was in preserving and keeping in memory those events that had some importance for the people at large. By and by the aims changed.

(ii) Aims of Teaching History in the 19th Century: Nineteenth century saw the development of scientific outlook in the various aspects of life. Teaching of history was now based on scientific outlook. It aimed at reviving the past events of the society with a view to help the present day set-up.

With the development of the democracy and nationalism, teaching of history assumed a different outlook. It is now thought to be an integral part of education. Karl Auguste and Muller made a good deal of efforts in this direction. These educationists thought that history should help the understanding of other subjects of studies. They have laid down the following, as the aims of teaching of history:

(a) Understanding the present in a better manner, with the help of the study of the past;

(b) Bringing about the intellectual development of the children, and

(c) Helping the study and understanding of other subjects.

(iii) Aims of Teaching History in Modern Times. Today, we see that there are definite aims laid down for the teaching of history. These aims are based on scientific outlook. Various thinkers and scholars have tried to assess and study aims of teaching of history. These aims are briefly as under:

Aims According to Miss Drummond

Miss Drummond in her book *history in schools* has tried to make a thorough study of the aims and objectives of the study of history. She has laid down the following aims for the study of history:

(a) Interest for the Study of History: The first aim of the teaching of history is to create interest in the future. The history, in fact,

is a treasure of knowledge so its study can be quite useful for young children.

To stabilise interest of students in the study of history we need very capable and devoted teachers who are able to link the past with the day-to-day life of the present.

(b) Formation of Scientific Attitude: One of the aims of teaching history is the development of scientific attitude in the student. To develop such an attitude the vast historical data should be used in a scientific way.

(c) Development of International Outlook and Understanding: Since at present we live in an era of international understanding and outlook so to be able to live we must be prepared to understand the outlook of the people of other countries. This should, therefore, be one of the aims of teaching of history.

Many other scholars have also laid down the aims of the teaching of history. There may be summarised as under:

(i) Utilitarian Aim. Like any of the subject the study of history helps us in earning bread and butter and so it is one of the main aims and we study history to earn our livelihood. History helps us to grow out of narrow outlook and enables us to take a proper place in life.

(ii) Intellectual Aim: The basic aim of education is to bring about an all round development of the personality of the child. It includes the intellectual development as well. In this respect we reproduce the remarks of *F.C. Hoppold*, "Study of history results in clear and vivid form, freedom from bias and irrational prejudices, ability to think and argue logically, and to form aim independent judgment supported by the evidence which is available and at the same time, the realisation that every conclusion must be recorded as a working hypothesis to be modified or rejected in the light of fresh evidences".

The correct picture in this respect is presented in the following extract.

"It (history) trains memory and power of concentration. It improves the reasoning and judgment of pupils by presenting facts in logical sequence and by providing opportunities for weighing evidence and for shifting the right from the wrong."

(iii) *Social and National Aim*: Through the study of history, it is accepted that the students will develop the spirit of sociality and sociability and the knowledge acquired by history will, help them to know what their forefathers have done. They will also know how their forefathers tried to raise the social status and help their fellowmen. That was an age of social interaction and social get-together.

The following quotation quite clearly presents the social aim of the study of history:

It is a broad and human patriotism that develops rational humanity rather than overbearing audiciousness and it is desired to perpetuate the principles of justice and humanity that control the life of a nation.

(iv) *Moral Aim*: Study of history also aims to develop the qualities of morality in the educants, it is the duty of the teacher to acquaint the students with the lives and deeds of great men of the past. Sacrifices and noble deeds of great men shall inspire the young souls to acquire those moral qualities that are helpful in raising the society and its values. It has rightly been remarked:

"But the teacher must not regard history as a series of object lessons in morality, and must realise the danger that children may also see how wicked have flourished in past and are still flourishing. The moral aim, therefore, cannot be overemphasized."

Aims of Teaching History According to Prof. Linwood Chase

According to Prof. Linwood Chase, the aims of teaching history are as follows:

(1) To collect the data pertaining to history.

(2) To evaluate the contributions of the past.

(3) To develop the consciousness in the pupils about society and social values.

(4) To help the students in having a correct idea about the importance and meaning of liberty and freedom.

(5) To help the students to understand the influence of historical facts and situations upon life.

(6) To develop the spirit of patriotism.

(7) To help the students to understand the series of social changes and their importance in social progress.

(8) To inculcate the interest of the pupils in the study of history and to encourage them to have a proper idea of time, place and their relationship.

(9) To understand the sequence of historical events since ancient times.

(10) To have a clear idea of historical facts and to give them a shape in order to have their practical utility.

(11) To study the development of human race.

Objectives of Teaching History

The objectives are the specific and precise behavioural outcome of teaching a particular topic in history. Any topic in history helps in realising some general aim of teaching history. The two important characteristics of a good objective are:

(i) It should be specific and precise and

(ii) It should be attainable.

Bloom's Taxonomy of Objectives

Bloom's taxonomy of objectives is a classification of instructional objectives in a hierarchy. According to it the specific objectives have been classified into the following three categories:

(a) cognitive domains objectives,

(b) affective domains objectives, and

(c) psychomotor domains objectives.

The cognitive domain objectives include knowledge, understandings, applications, analysis, synthesis and evaluation.

The affective domain objectives include the appreciations, values, attitudes, interests and feelings.

The Psychomotor domain objectives include skills.

Now an attempt will be made to briefly discuss these objectives.

1. Knowledge of Objectives

To impart knowledge in the basic aims of education and so it naturally is the basic aim of teaching of any subject including history. By imparting knowledge of history to the student it is expected that he acquires a knowledge of the following:

(i) The student acquires knowledge of terms, concepts, events, facts, ideas, trends, movements, related to historical phenomenon, e.g., Recalls terms, recognises, reads maps, locates maps, charts etc.

(ii) Acquires comprehension of terms, concepts etc., e.g., translates mutually different forms of communication, differentiates, compares and contrasts, classifies and classifications, expands and summarises, illustrates, detects and rectifies errors, interpolates and extrapolates the required information.

(iii) Applies knowledge to unfamiliar situations e.g., selects facts, concepts etc., establishes relationships, employs known procedures in new situations, restructures given materials, predicts outcomes restates problems in new perspectives.

(iv) Developes critical and creative thinking, e.g., discovers difficulties involved, detects the logical fallacies, hypotheses, verifies, infers, generalises, evaluates, writes historical fiction

(v) Developes practical skills in the field study of history e.g., improvises tools and apparatuses, prepares models, draws maps and charts, reserves specimens and exhibits, manipulates things, organises display of exhibition etc.

2. Affective

(i) Developes desirable attitudes, e.g. develops a sense of patriotism, becomes open minded and receptive, developes social virtues accepts civic responsibilities developes feelings of national integration and international understanding, realises the importance of international co-operation and piece and justice, values human rights and privileges, evaluates social changes critically.

(ii) Developes interests and appreciations, e.g. reads voluntarily and appreciates literature and fiction of historical type, e.g. collects relevant materials, produces display material, discusses in historical perspective the social, political, economic and educational problems, visits places of historical interests, writes articles and fiction on subjects of historical importance.

The psychomotor domain objectives include skills.

Some of these objectives are attained at various stages of education and the objectives of teaching of history at primary stage, at higher secondary stage of education are given here:

Objectives of Teaching History at the Primary Stage

At this stage of education the main objectives of teaching history to pupils are:

(i) *To Develop in the Students the Interest for History:* For achieving this aim it is desirable that the pupil is not burdened with a lot of information. He should not have a fear of examination.

(ii) *Development of the Power of Imagination*: The power of imagination which is an essential characteristic of childhood can be developed through teaching of history. This can be achieved by using story-telling method. Since pupil are quite fond of stories so it is quite natural for them to get interested in history if they are taught by story-telling method.

(iii) *To Make Students Conscious of the Influence of Past on Their Present Life*: It is desirable to develop in students the sense of time and this can be achieved with the help of time charts, time curves, time graphs and their frequent use in the teaching of history.

(iv) *To Develop Spirit of Patriotism and World-Brotherhood*: While teaching history an attempt be made to inculcate in the pupils a sense of patriotism and world-brotherhood.

Objectives of Teaching History at the Junior High School Level

Teaching of history to the students of the Junior High School level shou'd be done with the following objectives in mind:

(1) The real interest in the history should be developed in the students.

(2) Various mental facalties of the children should be developed.

They should be encouraged to take up independent thinking. Critical faculty should be developed in them. They should be encouraged to look at various historical facts from a critical point of view.

(3) The students should be encouraged to look at the present in the light of the past, and also to dream future.

(4) The sense of time, as developed at the primary stage, should be further developed. More abstract means should be employed to develop this sense of time.

(5) Patriotism and world-brotherhood should be developed in greater respect.

Objectives of Teaching History at the Higher Secondary Level

At the Higher Secondary level, teaching of history should be carried on with the following objective in view:

(1) Interest in the study of history, as developed at the primary and junior stages, should be strengthened and consolidated.

(2) Mental faculties of the students should be so developed that they may acquire the power of reasoning and arriving at the decisions. The students should be encouraged to examine things critically and accept them only when their power of reasoning accepts them.

(3) The students should be given idea of the exchange of the various cultures of the world. They should be made to realise that every country of the world has to depend upon the other with regard to its culture in one way or the other.

(4) The students should be encouraged to judge the present in the light of the past. They should also be made capable of looking forward.

(5) They should be acquainted with the 'Law of Cause and Effect.'

(6) Their sense of time, as developed at the primary and junior stages of education, should be strengthened and consolidated. A scientific outlook should be developed in them.

(7) An attempt be made to acquaint the students with the social, political and religious problems of society and their possible solutions.

(8) An attempt be also made to teach them about the development of the civilisation of the world.

2.3 VALUES OF TEACHING HISTORY

We have already seen a relationship between *aims* and *objectives*. Aims are nothing but set objectives according to which the teacher acts. The **values** are the gains of those aims. Actually speaking the values are achieved when the aims are acquired. So we can say that aims are, in itself, where as the values are the product.

An analysis of aims and objectives of teaching of history reveals that its study will not lead to any materialistic gains. Its value is cultural, humanising and disciplinary. The study of history leads to development of the understanding of the cultural heritage, provides the pupil some intellectual training and inculcates in them moral virtues. It also arouses in pupils a patriotic fervour.

Following are a few values of teaching history:

(1) Though history, an attempt is made to enrich the knowledge of the students on the basis of the past experiences. An attempt is also made to develop the spirit of sympathy and self-confidence.

(2) It leads to the intellectual development of the child. The child tries to employ his intellect in the solution of various problems. Children, when they study the deeds of great heroes like Rana Pratap, Shivaji or Razia Begum, feel to be like them. If this thinking could be given a practical shape, it shall be very useful for the students and the society at large.

(3) through the teaching of history, an attempt is made to inspire the students to achieve great deeds.

(4) Teaching of history also strengthens the relationship between the teacher and the taught.

(5) It develops in the students the qualities that may help them to adjust themselves with society.

(6) Teaching of history can generate, in the students, the interest of studying the deeds of great men. This interest helps them to employ their leisure in the study of the lives of great men and women. With this study, their feelings are directed towards the high ideals and values.

(7) Through the study of history it is possible to develop effectiveness in our life.

(8) Serious students of history can develop the qualities of partiotism, ideal citizenship and service for the motherland. It is possible for the students to develop all these qualities when the teacher has given a real turn to their interest and talents.

(9) It develops the power of reasoning and thinking in the pupils.

(10) It also developes, in the pupils, the quality of objectivity and impartiality. It encourages them to undertake the service of mankind without any self-interest.

REVISION QUESTIONS

1. "Teaching of History in our high school can be used for developing civic and moral sense in the students." Discuss fully.
2. What aims of teaching History in India Schools be specially emphasised by the teacher in the present socio-political conditions of our country? Give sound arguments to justify your answer.
3. What are the aims of teaching history at the secondary school stage ? What changes will you suggest in the context of present political and socio-economic changes ?
4. Write a short essay on the "Aims of Teaching History to class VIII".
5. Discuss briefly the values of teaching History in our schools.
6. What are the aims of teaching History to higher classes in our secondary schools? How are these aims sought to be achieved through the present syllabus in History, prescribed for the secondary schools in your state ?

Chapter 3

Correlation of History with Other Subjects

3.1 INTRODUCTION

The major aims of education in the unification of knowledge existing in different branches of learning. To achieve such a unification a conscious effort has to be made by teachers teaching various subjects. It is only by such a joint venture that we will be able to achieve the goal of unification of knowledge and bridge the gap that separates them.

3.2 IMPORTANCE OF CORRELATION

No subject can be taught in isolation particularly History. To take the learning process to its devised and we have to take full advantage of various correlations and applications of history. Just for our convenience we have divided history in different branches of study. However, a conscious effort is made now-a-days to integrate various branches of history and to treat the subject as a synthetic whole. Teaching of history is done keeping in view its correlation with other subjects. It helps the students in understanding of subject matter by the students. It is possible to correlate different experiences and at the same time, allow different aptitudes and incluciation to work with co-ordination and correlation. The unit of the students works in such a manner that he can understand a subject that is being taught, keeping in view its correlation with other subjects. Such a teaching brings about a healthy development of personality.

The various meanings given to correlation can be summarised in the following words:

"By correlation" we do not mean only to mix one subject to the other but it is a sphere by which we understand that knowledge grows as a whole and it is, therefore, neither possible nor desirable to teach any subject in inter tight compartments."

In the opinion of Grim, "The division of knowledge has produced an unnatural difference between the two subjects, the unification of the two is essential to enliven the taste for knowledge".

Writing about correlation Guyas writes, "Facts and ideas have real and useful influence over the mind only when we systematise and co-ordinate them which facts and ideas, as they are produced."

Types of Correlation

There are three important types of correlation. A brief description of these is given as follows:

(1) *Incidental Correlation:* While teaching when the teacher tries to establish co-relation of a particular topic of the subject with some other topics of some other subject, it is called an incidental correlation. It is not a planned one. The teacher does not make a conscious and systematic attempt to correlat the teaching of the topic with the other topics of the other subject. If the teacher is studious and learned, such an incidental correlation is bound to take place.

(2) *Conscious or Systematic Pre-planned Correlation*: In such a correlation, the teacher has to plan it in, his mind beforehand. In order to establish such a correlation, teacher has to make some study. For example, if the teacher wants to teach the history of Indus Valley Civilization, he has to explain the climate and the effect of the climate on the civilization before telling about the development and the downfall of the Indus Valley Civilization.

(3) Concentric Correlation: Here an attempt is made to establish correlationship between the various branches and topics of teaching of history.

3.3 CORRELATION OF HISTORY WITH OTHER SUBJECTS

The social education is nothing but a short course of history, depicting social, economic, industrial, scientific and cultural aspects of man's life. It throws light on the inter-dependence of man and man, nation and nation and country and country.

In view of Dr. Terevelyan, "History is not a subject at all but a house in which all subjects dwell." In Ziller's opinion, " History is the central subject round which all other subjects can revolve". Prof. Johnson opines, "History with or without the name, certainly has been and is a background for other social sciences. History may indeed be regarded as the only field in which all other social sciences meet".

Expressing his views on this, Koerner says, "Occupying as it does an intermediate position between the humanities and social sciences and employing both the qualitative approach of the humanist and the quantitative data of the behaviourist, it serves as a medium through which student can learn some thing of literature and arts on the one hand, and politics, economics and social behaviour on the other".

Due to the above stated facts history can be easily related to other subjects.

1. Correlation of History with Literature

History of development of literature is a part of history at large. Imagination which is an essential part of literature, imparts human touch to the teaching of history. It is only by "interpreting his sentiments and feelings as they are expressed in literature that the study of either literature or history can be made vital". History provides material, inspiration and background of contemporary events and conditions to literary persons. In its turn literature throws a light on popular taste, moral and intellectual standards, prejudices, ideals and inspirations of a nation. So both history and literature are closely correlated subjects.

2. Correlation of History with Language

A thorough knowledge of language is quite essential to have a thorough knowledge of any subject. While teaching languages various stories are taken out from different pages of history. Students are quite frequently required to write essays on topics of historical importance.

Oral and written expression is also very essential. In teaching history we provide opportunities to the students for discussing, speaking, debating, paper reading as also of narrating their experiences in black and white. Thus, we find a lot of correlation existing between history and language.

3. Correlation Between History and Geography

History in intimately correlated to Geography and in 50's the two subjects were taught together. In fact they are twins, one stresses time and the other space. History studies people of different times and geography deals with the people of different places.

The two subjects are now studied separately for convenience of study but we cannot completely separate the two subjects. In the words of **Prof. Immanuel Kant**, "Geography and history fill up the entire circumference of our perceptions, geography, that of space and history that of time." No history can be complete without some reference to space. Similarly no geographical account can be intelligible without reference to development in timê. So both history and geography are concerned with the inter-play of human and physical factors.

Geography is the stage on which drama of history is enacted and it is the geography which determines the historical events and can offer explanation for historical actions of mankind. Similarly historical facts can serve as a good basis for arousing interest in geographical studies. In explanation of historical fact geographical factors are taken into consideration. Various factors taken into consideration are physical conditions of the life of man, climate, means of communication etc. All these factors determine the direction of human life and history increased by human life and his activities. History of each and every country is governed by there factors. Truly speaking historical studies desired of geographical background would be inaccurate and unscientific.

The story of man's evolution since primitive stage, cannot be told without the varied geographical settings of the world. Man's mode of living, dieting and dressing etc., are all determined by his physical environment.

If England grew into a powerful nation and acquired a rich history, it was very much due to its geographical conditions. Geographical factors were the sole cause of the down fall of many empires. The growth of Delhi, Lahore or Landon can be better understood by considering various geographical factors. The history of hostility between France and Germany can be explained on the basis of existence of river Rhine and Lorrain coal-fields.

The correlation between history and geography becomes quite

evident if we look at the equipments/apparatus used for teaching of these subjects. For teaching these subjects we make use of maps, pictures and atlases.

4. Correlation Between History and Civics

Till quite recently, civics was thought to be a part of history. It is now treated as a separate subject but there is a direct correlation between the two. Civics describes the pattern of administration of present day while history gives an account of the pattern of administration that existed in the past. The knowledge of civics cannot be obtained without reference to history. Even constitution is an outcome of the long history behind it. It is history that guides the actions and foundations of the government. In the words of Prof. Johnson, "The study of history in schools has, from beginning in large past, been a study of the forms of the government, of changes in government and of actions by the government, civil government can best be studied as a part of history". Again it is history that describes the progress of human ideas and institutions through the ages. It is history from that we get an up-to-date knowledge about the origin, development and progress or decline of some of the social institutions. Thus, there is close relationship between the two subjects.

5. Correlation Between History and Economics

Economics is the study of wealth which deals primarily with production, distribution, consumption and exchange. But this study is in relation to man and his daily life activities. Thus a correlation between history and economics is quite natural. Economic conditions play a vital role in the course of history. If a country could attain a height of civilization in a period, it must have been because of good economic conditions of a country or various countries in various periods. To know the economic conditions of India during reign of Akbar or Shahjahan we shall have to go through the pages of history. In history we are also told that certain empires faced liquidation only because of economic reasons.

Similarly, the course of economic events have been influenced by historical circumstances, e.g. Mohd. Tughlak had certain plans, but the historical conditions of his time did not favour them and so he could not succeed, however, afterwards these plans were considered to be good and scientific.

So we find a close correlation between history and civics. They are as well as supplementary.

6. Correlation Between History and Art

Art activities are quite intimately related to history. In history students are required to draw pictures, battle-plans, graphs, maps' time lines and time charts etc. They are also required to prepare models of buildings, costumes and stage scenery for dramatic performance. This type of teaching aids are a must for the teaching of history. All these aids are the products of Art and crafts. Thus, art provides a base to teaching of history. It also makes the subject interesting and delightful.

Art is the practical application of the scientific knowledge. This practical application can be of two types: *(a)* Utilitarian, and *(b)* Fine.

Whether the art is utilitarian or fine, it presents a picture of the things. Various events of history are presented before our eyes in the form of pieces of art. The paintings of Ajanta and Ellora are presented through art. Taj Mahal represents the whole reign of Shahjahan. It very clearly indicates the history of the economic conditions of that period. Coins, arms and other pieces of art are helpful in ascertaining the history of that period.

The history of development of art forms the subject-matter of history. What was the condition of the art during Gupta period or Buddha period or Mughal period can be known to us only through history. Had there been no history, we would not have learnt about the various styles of art.

In short, both these subjects are inter-linked.

7. Correlation Between History and Physical Sciences

Though no direct relationship is apparent between history and physical sciences but indirectly there is a definite correlation between the two. All the principles and theories of science are based on facts and these are found out after a good deal of scientific study. But the knowledge as to how these principles evolved, developed and came into actual practice, can be acquired through the study of history. Thus, it is history that gives us a picture of the development and progress of science. The development of science takes a long period and it may take generations and centuries to evolve and reach perfection. It is only through the knowledge of history that the work done by one generation is known to other generation. It is history that tells us how much has actually been done and what still remains to be done. This history teacher is working very closely with the science teacher when he is tracing the history of a scientific invention, narrating the biography of an eminent scientist or describing the impact of scientific development on human society. In fact, advances in science and technology, as applied to human life, have revolutionised our social relationships to a great extent, in the present-day world.

8. Correlation Between History and Mathematics

The relationship between history and Mathematics is reciprocal. History helps mathematics to know about various mathematicians who were pioneers in their field and enriched mathematics by their contributions. History also provides the information about the origin and development of mathematics.

Mathematics helps history in regards to calculation of dates and days etc. of various historical events.

Acquisition of time sense in history is based on the knowledge of mathematics. These two subjects are complementary to each other. Really, speaking, there is a vast difference between the two subjects. Mathematics is generally called a dry subject, while history is supposed to be an interesting subject. But the knowledge of history can make teaching of mathematics quite interesting.

9. Correlation Between History and Theology

History and theology are intimately related. Religion has influenced the course of history to a very great extent. In older times, it was the religion that guided people to make conquests and fight certain battles that have now become a part of the history. Many of the wars and political upheavals were caused by religious feelings. Therefore, the knowledge of theology is very helpful for a historian. Without the knowledge of theology, it is difficult to have a thorough knowledge of history.

Similarly the knowledge of history is also helpful for the knowledge of theology. The birth and growth or the establishment and foundation of various religions and sects are studied under history. The causes of failure and success of various religions form the subject matter of history. It is the history that gives us the knowledge about the spread and importance of religion in a certain period or certain periods.

In short, it may be said that both the subjects are intimately related.

10. Correlation Between History and Sociology

Sociology has a wide scope of study. It studies the development of the human society at large. Really speaking, the subject-matter of history, geography, civics, political science etc., could very safely be included within the broad scope of the study of sociology. In fact, sociology gives us knowledge of the development of the society. It aims at developing man into an ideal social being History is very helpful in acquiring the knowledge of the development of society under various periods and under various conditions. The teaching of history should invariably be guided by the knowledge of sociology. Similarly, study and teaching of sociology can draw a lot from the knowledge of history.

11. Correlation Between History and Handwork

There is a definite relation between history and handicraft. While teaching history, we make use of models, charts, pictures, toys etc. Teaching aids are an essential part of the teaching of history. These aids are the product of craft or hand-work. Thus, hand-work provides a lease of the teaching of history.

The most important educational slogan of the day in '*learning by doing*' and doing involves hand-work. The involvement of hand-work in teaching of history helps to co-ordinate the activities of hand and mind. thus correlation of hand-work and history is not only good for the general development of child's mind but it is also quite effective in teaching of history.

Thus, we find a close correlation between history and hand-work.

REVISION QUESTIONS

1. "History is a subject which is closely correlated with other social sciences." discuss this statement.
2. What is the importance of correlating the teaching of history with other school subjects ? Discuss with illustrations.
3. How can history be taught effectively, correlating it with other school subjects ? Give examples.
4. Discuss the relationship of history with Geography and Economics and state how far these subjects can be helpful in making History teaching more effective and functional.
5. Can Physical Science and Mathematics be helpful to the teaching of history ? State your views with examples.

Chapter 4

Classification of History

4.1 INTRODUCTION

History in the story of the progress of mankind since times immemorial. If history is taken from this point of view we can easily conclude that there is one history of the whole world and such a history could only be world history. However, for the convenience of study historians have divided history into various parts or branches. Every such part is complete in itself. No one can be called a true historian if he has read only a part of this long and varied journey of the progress of mankind. A true historian is one who has read all the branches of history.

4.2 BASIS OF CLASSIFICATION

1. Classification of history on the basic of space or geographical boundaries.

On this basis history is classified as:

(a) World history,

(b) National history,

(c) Provincial or regional history, and

(d) Local history.

2. Classification of history an the basis of time or period

On this basis history is classified as:

(a) History of early ages,

(b) Ancient history

(c) Medieval history, and

(d) Modern history.

3. Classification of history on the basis of circumstances

On this basis history is classified as:

(a) Political history,

(b) Economic history, and

(c) Social history.

4.3 STUDY OF A PARTICULAR BRANCH OF HISTORY

On the basis of classification given above history is taught at different levels. A brief description of these is given here.

1. World History

When should we teach the world history to our students? Various educationists have given their opinion and there are two prominent schools of thought on this question:

One is of the opinion that it should not be taught to the children at the lower stages of education. This is meant only for the students of higher classes.

The Second School of Thought is of the opinion that the student must be given a glimpse of the world history. This is not likely to be difficult for them. On the other hand, they shall evidence curiosity in it. They shall also acquire acquaintances with the ways of living of the people of the other countries. This view is based on the Child psychology. These thinkers also believe that while presenting a picture of the history of the world to the children, an attempt should be made to start this at the earliest possible ages to awaken greater curiosity in the students.

Now educationists have come to realise that at the secondary level of education history should be taught in the background of world history, however, such a background should be sketchy only and should not go into details of world history.

Since it will not be possible to take up world history at the elementary school stage because of the fact that at this stage the students are too young to understand things or even events beyond their immediate social and physical environment. At this stage we can teach them the biographies of some prominent "world figures" or great men of the world. At the middle stage we can introduce the study of certain important social and religious movements. Finally a comprehensive course of world history in a sketchy form be taught at the higher secondary stage.

2. National History

Nation is a geographical, social and political entity of the world the similar units in a country are known as regions for the purpose of historical studies. However, such a view may not be quite useful in the present age of internationalism. It is this desirable to introduce the study of national history or regional history in such a way that it does not develop regionalism or provincialism in them

V.A. Smith, a famous British historian has described India as "an ethnological museum in which numberless races of mankind may be studied". However, through all these diversities, these runs a strong invisible under-current of unity that nourishes and sustains the tremendous variety. This is India's cultural unity. While ancient cultures of other countries such as Egypt, Mesopotamia, Rome and Greece etc., are now mere memories and have no direct link with the life of the present generation in these countries, our ancient culture and civilization have survived through the ages and still have direct bearing on our present day life. This is the most notable feature of our history. As Dr. A. C. Majumdar says, "Indian history and institutions form an unbroken chain by which the past is indissolubly linked with the present".

Though we have varieties of traditions which differ from state to state and each state has a history of its own. It is the duty of the history teacher to present a comparative picture of these various histories but always keeping in mind to not let the unity or spirit of oneness slip of his hands.

3. Regional History

Regions are the similar units in a country. Inspite of the fact that such a study of history may be desirable and useful it is more likely to prove harmful.

The usefulness of such a study lies in the fact that each region (e.g. In case of India, Punjab, Rajasthan, Andhra Pradesh, Kerala etc.) have got their fascinating history. Different sages and seers, political leaders, social reformers from across the country have kept alive the great traditions of Indian culture and civilisation in their respective areas, however, their teachings never remained confined to any particular area or region but effected Indian life as a whole.

4. Local History

Though the term in self-explanatory but in history it does not necessarily mean only the history of a town or village in which the child lives. It definitely includes the history of the suburbs and the neighbourhood with which the child is familiar. The materials in and around his neighbourhood will stimulate more interest in the child and it could be a profitable starting point in the teaching or history. Though there exist innumerable monuments and other sources of historical importance throughout the length and breadth of our country but only resourceful teachers can make a full use of these in teaching effectively many of the important topics and events of national or provincial history. It is the duty of the history teacher to familiarise this students with their immediate surroundings and make the fullest possible use of such information in further enrichmemt of their knowledge of history.

Importance of Local History

The various advantages of teaching local history can be summarised as under:

(i) The children became acquainted with the local customs and traditions which broaders their out look.

(ii) It is quite interesting to the students because it is related to their ancestors.

(iii) It develops in students emotional feelings towards their religion and they become interested to work for its development.

(iv) It develops in students a scientific out look.

(v) Local surveys give valuable training in history. These are as useful as laboratory work in the teaching of science.

(vi) It helps in the development of skills and right attitudes.

Writing about the importance of local history, E.S. Hasluck, "The study of Local history is of real importance and should most certainly find some space, however, small, in the school history syllabus. It helps and brings home to the pupil, by everyday contact with historical scenes, names and buildings, the sense of the development which his country has undergone, and removes his thoughts from time to time away from the present to the contemplation of the ages that are passed".

Teaching of Local History at Different Stages of Study

It is true that the Local history is of great importance, but the teacher should not wholly depend upon the Local history. It should serve just to illustrate and illuminate National or International history. It should be taken as supplementary study. Local history is of great importance to the students of primary classes as well as to the student's of junior classes. It teachers the boys to respect the customs and traditions of that place because they are germs of the life of the citizens. Due emphasis should be given to the Local history at the primary and higher secondary stages. However, in the higher classes, Local history is not so much important. It must be taught but it shall not be of great use for the students of these classes. At the higher secondary stage, the students should be asked to take excursion to the nieghbouring places. They should be encouraged to collect materials from the different parts of the locality which are of historical importance. The students must know about the historical buildings of their locality and their impact upon the social life. They should be encouraged to collect models, specis, coins etc., and take pictures of the different material of historical importance.

Method of the Study of Local History

While teaching Local history, the following methods may be employed:

(1) Excursions and tours should be arranged for the places that have importance in the Local history.

(2) An attempt should be made to present a history of the local community and social groups.

(3) An attempt should also be made to present before the students, a history of the various changes that have taken place in the locality, in political, social and economic life.

(4) Students should be encouraged to have a look at various places of historical importance in the locality.

(5) They should be encouraged to have knowledge of the history of the names of the roads of the locality.

(6) During the teaching of history of higher classes, the teacher should often refer to Local history for illustrating the influence of the past on the present and to make clear how

present is the product of past.

from the above discussion we conclude that local history can become a valuable aid both to the teacher and the student of history.

4. History of Early Ages (Ancient History)

It includes the history of stone age. In those days the life was difficult and it was quite difficult to get food, clothing, dwelling units etc. He lived in open space, resorted to hunting for his food and used barks of trees or skin of animals to cover his body. This story of man's life in different parts of the world is quite interesting to the children and enables them to understand how civilisation has developed through the ages. After the stone age started the ancient age when man began to settle in social groups. He started performing certain religious and social acts and it led to the classification of society into various categories. During this period some ard ant literature also developed. The scene was dominated by heroes and warriors.

5. History of the Middle Age or Mediaeval Ages

During this period human civilisation progressed a good deal. From the Indian point of view, this is called the period of Rajputs and Muslims. So far as the religious conditions are concerned, it was the age of multifarious religions. It will not be wrong to call it a period of religious and political activities.

6. Modern Period

Modern period is the period of the highest development of culture and civilisation. Various political, social, economic and religious changes have taken place during this period. Science, literature, art, etc., have worked wonders. It shall not be wrong to call it an Age of science. It is an Age of Space Conquest. Man has established his supremacy not only over the nature but over the space as well. Every day the train of progress is going ahead. Modern history deals with all these things.

7. Political History

In the opinion of Freeman, a great historian, history is essentially a record of political events because political events greatly influence the life of a community. But history must not remain only a record of political events. It must throw light on all aspects of community life the study of all aspects of political history not only satisfies the human curiosity but it also enable the students to have a knowledge of political events of the past. However, it should not be studied in a narrow manner, i.e., the deads of the rulers and the political changes should not be the only concern of the political history.

8. Economic History

While emphasising the importance of economic needs as the spring of all social conduct, Karl Marx has clearly laid down that *it is the economic condition that determines and influence the progress of society and human beings*. State, society, culture, art and literature etc., all depends upon economic circumstances. Since it all gives a central place to economic history so the study of economic history is very important.

Economic history should not be studied in isolation and an attempt be made to assess other types of events as well. We will come across many an instances in different period of history. When a powerful and strong willed ruler or conqueror appeared on the scene and brought about tremendous changes that greatly affected the social and economic life of the community.

9. Social History

It deals with the development of family and the related problems such as social organisations, traditions, education, agriculture etc. Thus, it is very wide subject and actually it indirectly deals with political history. It should be taught very cautiously and never in isolation.

10. Religious History

There is a class of educationists that lays great stress on the study of Religious history. It says that religion has influenced our civilisation and culture since the early ages. All the political and social events have taken place only on account of religion. Form this point of view, the study of Religious History is very important.

While studying Religious history, we should keep in mind that we do not look at religion from an universal and human point of view. It should be treated as a collection of virtues and good qualities that are helpful for the preservation of human race.

While teaching Religious History, the teacher has to be very cautions. He has to present things in a very objective manner. He should not criticise any religion because this is likely to hurt the susceptibilities of the followers of that religion.

REVISION QUESTIONS

1. What is the value of the local material in the teaching of history ? What are its various varieties and how would you use them at the higher secondary stage ?
2. In which period of Indian history, would your local history prove most useful to you as a history teacher in that locality ? Indicate clearly the use that you would make of it.
3. Classify history on the basis of the time, place and circumstances.

Chapter 5

Methods of Teaching History

5.1 INTRODUCTION

In order to achieve the aims and objectives of teaching of a particular subject certain maximum are laid down. The teaching of the subject is then planned and carried out keeping these maximum as the guiding principles. No doubt teaching is an art but the success of a teacher lies in making his subject so simple as to make it intelligible for his students.

In order to make children learn effectively, the teacher has to adopt the right method of teaching. **Method** is a procedure which teacher follows to make learning easy and effective. It is made up of various important steps. Many of these steps used in one method may also be used in other method. Generally speaking, method is the, "process of planning, guiding, sharing and evaluating learning with a group of students." It is, therefore, that the method is one of the most fundamental aspect of education and central problem of teaching.

Every teacher has got his or her own method of teaching. A method may be successful for one teacher but the same may not be successful with other teacher. A method should always be in accordance with the requirements of the age of students, their stages of education and their physical environments. A method should never be stereotyped. It should be workable and flexible. To be a successful teacher one should be familiar with all the methods of teaching but should be able to select one that suits him best at a particular time and place for directing and learning process.

Method of teaching history in the means by which knowledge of history is imparted to the students. In the words of C. P. Hill, "Method must be appropriate to the teacher's own personality, his gifts and his feelings; the teacher who has learned from the jawns of his students that they cannot tell a tale vividly must resist the temptation to plunge into narrative description, where as the teacher who has flair for swift black-board sketches, should make full use of them".

In this chapter an attempt will be made to discuss some common methods of teaching of history.

5.2 VARIOUS METHODS OF TEACHING OF HISTORY

Some of the important methods of teaching of history are as under:

(i) Story-telling method,

(ii) Biographical method,

(iii) Source method,

(iv) Text-book method,

(v) Laboratory method,

(vi) Problem method,

(vii) Project method,

(viii) Lecture method,

(ix) Self-study method,

(x) Discussion method, and

(xi) Unit method.

These methods will now be taken up for discussions are by one.

1. Story-telling Method

It is considered as the best method of teaching history at all stages, however, it is more useful at early stages of education i.e., elementary and primary stage of education. Since the students in elementary and primary classes are fond of listening to stories, so, if the teacher tell them about the lives of great men of various ages it definitely arouses their interest and provides a scope for imagination development. Plato laid much stress on story-telling method. The following points be kept in mind while using this method of teaching:

(i) Teacher should make sure that he has full control over the subject matter that he is likely to present in the form of a story.

(ii) His style should be natural and interesting.

(iii) He must know the art of acting and he should be able to lay stress on emotions as and when required.

(iv) While telling a story, there should not be too much of personal element in it.

(v) Teacher must always keep an eye on chronological order, and the sense of time and space.

Various Types of Stories

The stories being told to young children can mainly be classified as:

(i) True stories,

(ii) Myths, or

(iii) Legends.

True Stories. Such stories occupy a unique position in the teaching of history and are quite valuable in the teaching of history.

Myths. This refers to those stories that are mainly about fairies and other super-natural objects. Such stories are false and are of little or no historical value. As such they do not have much importance in the teaching of history.

Legends are those stories which do have certain elements of truth in them but their details are generally incorrect. The use of such stories can be made in junior and middle classes where we are not much concerned about the accuracy if details. In this regard we reproduce the words of Prof. Jarvis, "Truthfulnes should be the major criterion to guide as in taking the help of stories, while teaching history. Historical stories whether facts or legends, must be formulated by a truthfulness which is higher than mere accuracy of incidents".

Advantages of Story-telling Method

Some of the advantages of this method of teaching are as under:

(i) It enhances interest in the subject.

(ii) It helps in development of imagination.

(iii) It inculcates good virtues. Such virtues are likely to be inculcated in the students if they are told the life-stories of great men and women. Good virtues are truthfulness, charity, value, etc.

(iv) It provides inspiration for creative work.

2. Bio-graphical Method

Biography is the story of life of a great-man or woman. By using this method the great events of history can be taught as the events turning round the lives of great individuals. Teacher can make use of his method for inculcating in his students the values and ideals of life. Carlyle says, "The history of what man has accomplished in this world is at the bottom, the history of great man who have worked here."

This method is useful in primary classes and to some extent in secondary classes. Making use of this method teacher is in a position to put various historical facts in an interesting and lively manner. It is also helpful in motivation and can lead to the development of the qualities of patriotism and nationalism in the students.

Advantages of Biographical Method

Some of the advantages of this method are:

(i) It provides natural interest to students.

(ii) It is a simple method.

(iii) It is helpful to inculcate social and moral virtues.

(iv) It provides motivation to the students.

(v) It leads to the study of social life.

Limitation of Biographical Method

The major arguments against the use of this method are:

(i) It is undemocratic, because instead of laying stress as society it lays stress on a few great personalities.

(ii) It does not provide continuity of subject matter.

(iii) It tends to develop hero-worship.

(iv) It is not possible to teach complete history by this method.

(v) This method can not be used to teach world movements.

(vi) Many a times great ruler do not represent their times.

(vii) By adopting this approach it becomse difficult to follow the chronological order.

3. Source Method

It is a common knowledge that doing a certain thing is a better of learning it. Personally visiting a factory, a building, a mountain or a dam, is much better method of learning about them than merely reading or hearing about them. Similarly, the study and use of original material and original sources, will give a much better understanding of subject, like history, as compared to any other method. This is known as source method of teaching and learning history.

Source method is considered to be a very important method of teaching history. It helps the students of higher classes to construct a superstructure of historical facts with the helps of the source materials such as written cards, old chronicles, diaries, fermans, letters, contemporary documents, old inscriptions, statues, rains, battle-fields, pottery, tools, clothes, arms, armours, roads and bridges, monuments, building etc.

Classification of Sources

Historical sources are classified as under:

(i) *Archaeological sources*: e.g., monument finds, epigraphics, numismatics.

(ii) *Literary sources*: e.g., sacred or religious literature, secular, literature, foreign accounts.

(iii) *Oral traditions*, e.g., Local history etc.

They can also be classified as under:

(i) *Primary sources*, and

(ii) *Secondary sources.*

Important Sources of History

Some important sources of history are given below:

1. *Old Written Records*: These are the important sources of history. Written records comprise of old biographies, autobiographies, diaries, official despatches, letters, legal decrees, business documents, charters, accounts of journeys, religious books, accounts of kings and their courts written by old historians.

2. *Old Coins*: Old coins are very useful source of history. By these, we know about the dynasties and chronology. They also throw some light on the social conditions and development of art.

3. *Metal and Stone Inscriptions*: Indian kings issued grants of lands or cash *inams* to saints and other important persons. The orders

to the effect were inscribed on the copper plates and stones. So, they are also the source of ancient history.

4. Ancient Tools, Implements and Pieces of Pottery: So many tools, implements and pieces of pottery are buried in the olden ruins. They throw light on the civilisation of the ancient times. The study of these tools, implements and pieces of pottery also tell us the continuous story of the development of human race.

5. Inscription or Buildings, Rocks and Pillars: Inscriptions on old buildings, rocks and pillars also throw much light on the dim past. Ashoka's history is known to us from his inscriptions.

6. Ancient Buildings, Ruins and Monuments: These are the very important source of history. The ruins of Taxila and Mohanjodaro, the art works of Ellora and Ajanta and the old buildings of Delhi and Agra speak the glory of the ancient India.

7. Traditions Recorded in Literature: Old traditions recorded in literature and folk songs also throw light on what and how men thought and felt in the past.

How to Utilise Sources

The proper utilization of sources, which are available in such large numbers, is not an easy task. To make proper use of available sources the need of a "source book", is felt, which may be useful in the acquisition of knowledge of history. The following extract is this context in worth-noting.

"The original documents are too difficult, too technical and laborious to be properly interpreted and grasped. The paucity of such source books, however, cannot be over-looked."

Since students are not familiar with the purpose and utility of source material so it becomes the duty of the teacher to describe and explain such materials to students. For this purpose teacher can use same or more of the following ways:

1. Demonstration. The teacher should give an actual demonstration, to his students of the way in which a particular source can be utilised.

2. Assigned Reading. This can be achieved by the teacher if he asks some selected students to read certain selected passages that may be assigned to them.

3. *Problem Solving*. Problems can be easily solved by making use of source materials. Source materials help the student to reach the truth.

The use of source material can be made in the beginning of the lesson, during the lesson, at the end of lesson or even after finishing the lesson.

Importance of Sources

In the teaching of history various sources are quite important because of the following reasons:

(i) Sources are quite useful to make the history real and alive for the students.

(ii) Sources make history concrete and meaningful.

(iii) Sources help in stimulating the imagination of children.

(iv) Sources make the children research minded. They do not accept the facts without proper reasoning and analysis. In this way they become critical-minded.

(v) Sources supplement the text-book knowledge and make the lesson vivid. In this respect they act as visual aid in the teaching of history.

(vi) They reveal the nature of reliable evidence and give a sense of reality.

(vii) This provide functional knowledge.

Difficulties in Utilising Original Sources

Though there are various advantages in utilising original sources but there are a few limitations in the use of such original sources. Some of the difficulties are given below.

(i) Sources of real value are not available.

(ii) In case of Indian students there in the *problem of language*. Most of the original sources of historical or cultural value, are in languages, foreign to Indian students. (e.g., in English, Arabic, Persian etc.)

(iii) Conflicting views of different contemporary writers.

Importance of Source Method

This method is used by history teacher in a scientific background and on the basis of certain facts.

This method is more suitable for the students of secondary classes. It is quite useful for developing the power of thinking, reasoning and drawing inferences, in such students. A few important advantages can be listed as under:

(i) Sources reveal the nature or reliable evidence.

(ii) They give a sense of reality

(iii) They provide training in reasoning and judgment.

(iv) They provide functional knowledge.

Because of the above advantages source method in quite useful for a history teacher.

Limitations of Source Method

Some of the limitations of source method are as under:

(i) It cannot be used at the lower levels of education.

(ii) Even expert historian cannot interpret all the sources, so the teacher feels difficulty in making use of this method.

(iii) A great-skill on the part of teacher is needed for proper use of this method.

(iv) It is not a complete method.

(v) This method can not be used to teach all the topics in history.

(vi) It is a time consuming and expensive method.

4. Text-book Method

The text-book method is used for teaching of history event in great progressive countries. This method of teaching we revolve round the text-books.

In this method, the students are asked to learn certain facts given in a lesson of history book. They are asked to memorise and learn by heart some facts. The students may some times be asked to go through history textbooks and grasp the material given therein.

As with any method of teaching, this method also has its

advantages and shortcomings. Some of these are given here.

Advantages of Text-book Method

(i) It helps to develop, in the students, the efficiency to acquire knowledge by reading the books.

(ii) It encourages students to remain active and learn things by themselves.

(iii) It helps the students to know the length of answer to a particular question set in the examination.

(iv) It helps in developing the memory of the students.

(v) It gives an accurate account of the subject.

(vi) It suggests various application of the material.

(vii) It reflects and establishes standards.

(viii) It gives the teacher to expand or limit the size of a topic according to needs.

(ix) It can serve as basis of all other methods of teaching history.

(x) It presents to the student, different and opposing points of view as historical and current events.

Limitation of Text-book Method

(i) This method does not employ or use the maximum and principles of education.

(ii) This method narrows the out-look of students and they become inactive and lethargic. They do not take an active part in the acquisition of knowledge.

(iii) In this method the scope of revision is very much limited and the knowledge acquired by the students is not permanent.

(iv) This method does not develop the scientific out look in the pupils.

(v) It retards the originality in the students.

(vi) There past experience remain dormant.

(vii) This method leads to the development of cramming tendency in the students.

(viii) In case only are text-book is used by the teacher, then this method becomes even more rigid and unscientific.

(ix) Since the whole matter is condensed in a text-book there is a *possibility of error of details or of interpretation.*

(x) Text-books contain only minimum essentials.

5. Laboratory Method

In this method of teaching history is taught like a science subject. It is quite a new method for a country like India. However, this method is quite useful in imparting the knowledge of history to the students in a scientific manner. We came across the demand raised by history teachers of some countries that a laboratory be established for the study of history in a scientific manner. Such a laboratory should be equiped with the following apparatus :

(i) Table for practical and experimented work.

(ii) Black-board.

(iii) Radio.

(iv) Show Case

(v) Magic Lantern

(vi) Projector, screen etc.

(vii) Historical maps

(viii) Time curves and time-graphs etc.

(ix) Pictures of great rulers and persons etc.

In this method the teacher provides an outline of the work before the students and the students are required to fill the details from the knowledge they acquire through presentation.

Merits of Laboratory Method

(i) In this method the students acquire the knowledge as an active partner

(ii) It develops in the students the qualities of self-study and experimentation.

(iii) It is free from examination system as conducted at present.

Limitations of Laboratory Method

(i) It is quite expensive.

(ii) The knowledge that is acquired by the student, by this method, is not quite systematic.

(iii) The teaching by this method becomes quite mechanical.

6. Problem Method

As defined by C. V. Good, " The problem method is a method of instruction by which learning is stimulated by the creation of challenging situations that demand solution. It is a specific procedure by which a major problem is solved through the combined solution of a number of smaller related problems".

This method consists in training the pupils to solve problems. This method is based upon the process of finding out the results by attaching a problem in a number of definite steps. In this method the student is involved in finding out the answer to a given problem and terms actually it is a discovery method. In the words of Yoakam and Simpson, " a problem occurs in a situation in which a felt-difficulty to act is realised. It is a difficulty that is clearly present and recognised by the thinker. It may be purely mental difficulty or it may be physical and involve the manipulation of data. The distinguishing thing about a problem, however, is that it impresses the individual who meets it as needing a solution".

Procedure

The method proceeds in various steps discussed in the following lines :

1. Recognising the problem. First of all, we sense the presence of a problem and then identify the problem.

2. Defining the problem. The problem is then defined very precisely and accurately.

3. Collecting relevent data. Then all sorts or relevant data, which can be helpful in solving the problem, are collected and arranged in proper order.

4. Organising the data. Then the data is then organised in such a way that it can lead to the solution of the problem.

5. Formulating the tentative solution. On the basis of the organised data, the student formulates tentative solutions of the problem.

6. Arriving at the correct solution. Out of the tentative solutions, a correct solution is found out by a process of reasoning.

Merits of Problem-solving Method

(i) It prepares the students in problem-solving. This training is solving-problem is quite useful in solving problem in actual life.

(ii) It stimulates thinking, reasoning and imagination of the students.

(iii) It develops, a habit of doing work independently, in the students.

(iv) This method of teaching is quite suitable for history.

(v) It stimulates intellectual curiosity and motivates the students to exert further.

(vi) In this method there is ample scope for individual work as a student is free to solve as many problems as he likes.

(vii) It develops in the student a habit of self-study.

(viii) While learning by this method the student learns by doing and so the information is retained by him for a longer period of time.

(ix) There is a close teacher-pupil contact.

(x) It develops qualities such a patience, co-operation, self-confidence etc.

(xi) It provides to students a training in technique of information processing.

(xii) It helps to develop intellectual honesty in students.

(xiii) It provides the students a training in the methods and skills of discovering new knowledge in history.

Demerits of the Problem-solving Method

(i) It is a long drawn out and time consuming method.

(ii) It is not suitable for all topics in history.

(iii) This method is suitable only for bright and creative students.

(iv) This method is not suitable for students in lower classes.

(v) This method requires special preparation on the part of the teacher. An average teacher may find it difficult to adopt this method.

(vi) The content of history can not be organised according to

requirements of this method.

(vii) Suitable text-books for use of this method are not available.

Application

This method trains the pupils in problem-solving. They learn to sense, analyse, reflect, organise and solve the problems. It helps us at every step in our teaching-learning process. The teacher should carefully select the problems which are real and have definite educational values. The teacher should also prepare himself well for the success of the problem-solving method.

7. Project Method

This method was given by Dewey—the American philosopher, psychologist and practical teacher. The project method is direct outcome of his philosophy. According to Dr. Kilpatrick, "A project is a unit of whole hearted purposeful activity carried on preferably, in its natural setting". According to Stevenson "A project is problematic act carried to its completion in its natural setting". According to Ballard, " A project is a bit of real life that has been incorporated into the school".

The project method is not totally new. Project equivalent are advocated for the adolescent period by Rousseau in Emile (BK-III). A project plan is modified form of an old method called "concentration-of-studies." The main features of "concentration-of-studies plan" is that some subject is taken as the core or centre and all other school subjects as they arise are studied in connection with it.

Project method is based on the following principles:

(i) Learning by doing.

(ii) Learning by living.

(iii) Children learn better through association, co-operation and activity.

In this method, a project is taken which is then completed in a natural and social setting. As the project is carried to completion, the students learn so many things.

Procedure. Project method generally involves the following steps:

(i) *Providing a Situation*. The teacher provides a situation wherein the student feel like working on certain projects.

(ii) *Choosing*. Then the pupils are helped to choose project that islinked to their need.

(iii) *Planning*. Pupils then discuss how that project is to be executed? Steps of the procedure are planned and noted down.

(iv) *Executing*. The project is then executed as planned. Every body contributes his share of work.

(v) *Evaluating*. The project is then evaluated and possible knowledge is reviewed.

(vi) *Recording*. The knowledge gained is then recorded for future reference.

I. Providing a Situation

A project should arise out of a need felt by pupils and it should never be forced on them. It should be purposeful and significant. It should look important and must be interesting. For this the teacher should always be on a look out to find situations that arise discuss them with students to discover their interests. Situations may be provided by different methods. Some such methods may include talking to students on topics of common interest, e.g., how did they spend their holidays, what did they are in Delhi etc.

II. Choosing and Proposing

From various definitions of an educational project we get the same underlying ideas (a) School tasks are to be real and as purposeful as the tasks of wider life beyond the school walls. (b) They are of such a nature that the pupil is generally eager to carry them out in order to achieve a desirable and clearly realised aim.

According to Kilpatrick, " the part of the pupil and the part of the teacher, in most of the school work, depends largely or who does the proposing." The teacher should refrain from proposing by project otherwise the whole purpose of the method would be defeated. Teacher should only tempt the students for a particular project by providing a situation but the proposal for the project should finally come from the students. The teacher must exercise guidance in selection of the project and if the students make an unwise choice, the teacher should tactfully guide them for a better project. The essentials of a good project are:

(*i*) It should have evident worth for the individual or the group that undertakes them.

(*ii*) The project must have a bearing on a great number of subject and the knowledge acquired through it may be applicable in a variety of ways.

(*iii*) The project should be timely.

(*iv*) The project should be challenging.

(*v*) The project should be feasible.

It is for the teacher to see that the purpose of the project is clearly defined and understood.

III. Planning

The students be encouraged by the teacher to plan out the details of the project. In the process of planning teacher has to act only as a guide and he should give suggestions at times but actual planning be left to the students.

IV. Execution

Once the project has been chosen and details of the project have been planned, the teacher should help the students in executing the project according to the plan. Since execution of a project is the largest step in the project method so it needs a lot of patience on the part of the students and the teacher. During this step the teacher should carefully supervise the pupils in manipulative skills to present waste of material and to guard accidents. The teacher should assign work to different students in accordance with their testes, interests, aptitudes and capabilities. Teacher should see that every member of the group gets a chance to do some thing. Teacher should constantly check up the relation between the chalked out plans and developing project and as far as possible 'at the spot' changes and modification be avoided. However, it such changes become unavoidable these should be noted and reasons explained for future guidance.

V. Evaluation

The evaluation of the project should be done both by the pupils and the teacher. The pupils should estimate the qualities of what they have done before the teacher gives his evaluation. The evaluation of the project has to be done in the light of plans, difficulties in the execution and achieved results. Let the students have self-criticism and look through their own feelings and findings. This step is very useful because as a result of the project, the pupils can know the values of the information, interest, skills and attitudes that have been modified by the project.

VI. Record

A complete record of the project be kept by the students. The record should include every thing about the project. It should include the proposal, plan and its discussion, duties allotted to different students and how far were they carried out by them. It should also include the details of the places visited etc.

Role of Teacher

(i) In project method of teaching the role of it is that of a guide, friend and philosopher.

(ii) He helps the students in solving their problems just like an elder brother.

(iii) He encourages his students to seek collectively, amicably in the groups.

(iv) He also helps his students to avoid mistakes.

(v) He makes it a point that each member of the group contributes some thing to the completion of the project and in this process helps the sky and weaker students to work along with their class-mates.

(vi) If the students face failure during execution of some steps of the project the teacher should not execute any portion of the project but should only explain to his students the reasons of their failure and should suggest them some better methods or techniques that may be used by them next time for the success of the project.

(vii) During the execution step teacher also learns something.

(viii) Teacher should always remain alert and active during execution step and see that the project goes to completion successfully.

(ix) During execution of the project teacher should maintain a democratic atmosphere.

(x) The teacher must be well read and well informed so that he can help the students to the successful completion of the project.

Chief Characteristics of a Good and Successful Project

1. Usefulness. The project must be individually and socially valuable and must have a practical aim.

2. Maximum Number of Activities. It should provide many activities of various types. These should be quite suitable to pupils undertaking the project and should be able to draw the best from them.

3. Availability of Resources. The material connected with the project, should be readily available in or in the neighbourhood of the school. The pupils should be able to handle it without difficulty.

4. Economy. The project should not be expensive. It should give the best of results in the shortest possible time and with the least possible expense.

5. Beat Experience. It should provide experiences of a very high standard, including social contacts and character training. It must fulfill some educational purpose.

Examples of Projects in History

There are unlimited examples of projects that can possibly be used in teaching history. These may include field trips, school elections, making card-board, clay or wood models of various objects, writing plays based upon a period of history, preparing scripts for radio programmes, writing a song or a poem inspired by a historical event, dramatising events, making displays for the bulletin board, preparing pageants, arranging community surveys and starting a collection of old coins, stamps, specimens and other such things for the scrap-books and for the school museum.

Merits of Project Method

(i) It arouses interest of the pupils.

(ii) It provides knowledge in the integrated form.

(iii) The facts learnt are easily remembered.

(iv) There is an opportunity for mutual exchange of view.

(v) In this method the students is free to work according to his capacity.

(vi) It teaches the student the dignity of labour.

(vii) It helps in developing self-confidence and self-discipline in the student.

(viii) The project is not forced on the student nature it is chosen by him so they are motivated to learn.

Demerits of Project Method

(i) It does not provide the necessary drill work which is essential to have mastery of the topic.

(ii) It does not suit the fixed curriculum.

(iii) It is quite lengthy, time consuming and expensive method.

(iv) In this method there is a chance that some students may shirk work.

(v) Since each student has to perform certain specified duties for the completion of the project, the learning will not be uniform.

8. Lecture Method

It is the most commonly used method of teaching history. "It involves teaching by means of the spoken word." This method can be used at all levels of teaching.

This method is not quite suitable to realise the real aim of teaching history. In this method only teacher talks and the students are passive listeners. It is a teacher controlled method. The student is provided with a ready-made knowledge and because of this spoon feeding student loses interest and his powers of reasoning and observation get no stimulus. It shall be wise for the teacher to punctuate this method with question-answer method. He may put questions to the students sometimes as the material taught to them. This will keep the students alive to the subject-matter that is being taught to them.

Merit of Lecture Method

Lecture method commands certain merits. They are:

(i) It is less expensive.

(ii) It is time saving.

(iii) It is effective in providing information.

(iv) It is much inspiring.

(v) It is best tool for motivation.

(vi) It gives a sense of satisfaction to the students as well as the teacher. It gives them a feeling that they have learnt something.

Demerits of Lecture Method

Lecture method suffers from the following defects :

(i) It is teacher centered and not a students centered method.

(ii) It is oral and verbal.

(iii) It ignores the basic principle of learning by doing.

(iv) It does not develop scientific attitude and skill.

(v) There is no built in feed back.

(vi) It does not fulfill the needs and abilities of the individual students.

(vii) In this method ideas follow each other very rapidly and so it is not easy for students to comprehend the chain of the ideas properly, if their attention is diverted a little and if they miss one idea, they may not understand the whole topic at all.

(viii) This method does not keep teacher in contact with the students. There is no room for individual attention.

(ix) In this method the experimental side is totally neglected by the teacher.

(x) It is a kind of spoon-feeding and several faculties of students such as observation, independent thinking etc., get a little or no opportunity to grow.

9. Self-study Method

The basic aim of this method is to develop in pupils the habit of self-study. The teacher may ask the students to read a specific period or event of history and then he may ask questions on that lesson in the class. This helps the students in acquiring the knowledge independently. This is found to be a suitable method for teaching of history.

10. Discussion Method

The present age is an age of discussion. We arrive at a definite conclusion after thorough discussion. Discussion has now come to challenge the authoritarian methods through which education was imported in the old days " Discussion may take the form of a conference, a symposium or seminar. However, it should always be remembered that discussion is quite difficult and dangerous too. After a subject has been put to discussion it cannot be withdrawn. The main aim of discussion is to inculcate in students a habit of "group thinking" and "collective decision."

The essential parts of a discussion are:

(i) A leader,

(ii) A group,

(iii) A problem, and

(iv) A content.

We shall take up these one by one.

(i) The Leader. In our case the teacher is the leader. He has to prepare and conduct the discussion. For this he is required to put in a lot of labour and planning. Once the discussion has been initiated the teacher should act as a co-worker and a co-sharer. He should carefully watch the discussion while it is going on and should act as a prompt guide in case his pupils face any difficulty.

(ii) The Group. Students of the class of history form the group. All types of students (e.g., brilliant, average, below average etc.) are included in such a group. Teacher should make all out efforts to see that every member of this heterogeneous group participates in discussion.

(iii) The Problem. The topic under discussion in the class is the problem. It should be carefully selected and it should be made precise and exact. It should be such a topic that it is liked by the students and they consider it their own topic. For this end it is always advisable to involve the maximum number of students in the process of selection of topic for discussion. The topic selected must be real and functional and must be within the capacity and comprehension of the pupils.

(iv) The Content. It is the material of study and includes maps,

charts, picture, visual aids etc. Facts can be discussed only to prove them true or false. " Statements about value" can be discussed to establish their truth. It is about there statements that difference of opinion arises and discussion takes place.

Evaluation

Before closing the discussion each one participating in the discussion should evaluate to find if the discussion has added any thing to his knowledge or information, brought about any changes in his existing views, attitudes and prejudices etc. It is expected that after a successful discussion same changes must occur to make the participant a more active citizen.

Nature of Discussion

Discussion is neither a debate nor a declamation, its purpose is to share and weigh all conflicting interests or values. The participants in a discussion are "inter-related in a process of competitive co-operation" and "Agreement" is the declared purpose of discussion. Discussion is always organised in a disciplined atmosphere. A good discussion is actually a well planned and well mannered conversation and for this those participating in discussion are expected to the courteous, clear, good-natured, tolerant and scincere. To get desirable results from a discussion a healthy and informal climate during discussion is a must.

Advantages of Discussion Method

(i) It helps in collective decision-making.

(ii) It gives deep knowledge of the topic under discussion.

(iii) It inculcates the spirit of tolerance.

(iv) It leads to self-evaluation.

(v) It represents intellectual team-work.

This method of teaching history is useful at all levels. It is a very useful method because it enables the students to respect opinions and ideas of others, separate truth from falsehood, understand the topics, evaluate the findings and summarise the results. For this method to the successful it is essential that we have such teachers who are capable of providing guidance to the students.

11. Unit Method

In the teaching of history, unit has become the most popular form of organisation and the different ways of teaching it, are known as *unit method*. Unit method generally incorporates the use to both (problem and project) procedures.

In this method a particular topic is started in a particular class and finished over there, however, this method has failed to get approval from a majority of educational thinkers. In their opinion if this method is used, many irrelevant things may creep in and many relevant this may be left out. The students may be forced to study such things which are of no immediate importance to them. Moreover, if this method is adopted only a few tolrics will find a place in any particular class because all types of problems on that topic shall have to be solved by the students in one class. In the opinion of such educationists the *special method* of organisation of curriculum is preferable. In the spiral method a topic is divided into a number of small independent units to be dealt with in different classes that suit the mental capacities of the pupils. In there opinion such a method is more natural and less tiring to the students. To support it they argue that in such a method student loses nothing in accuracy and gains a lot of power of application of the general rules to particular problems.

The criterion of difficulty lays more emphasis on the fact that topics should be arranged in order of difficulty. But to take the topic as a unit is not a good arrangement. Topical arrangement is based on the unity of the topic i.e., exhaustion of the topic at the same time or at a stretch. However, it is unnatural and also impracticable to take a topic and exhaust all its possible portions and problems, simple as also complex, in the same class. For a good arrangement the following be kept in view:

(i) Every topic should be divided into parts.

(ii) These parts should be graded according to difficulty.

(iii) Each part should be introduced at a proper stage.

These different portions be allotted to be taught in different classes according to their difficulty and maturity of minds of pupils. Such an approach is called a *special approach.*

A portion is introduced when a sufficient background has been prepared for it. The remaining more tedious portions are left, for being taken up later on. Everything is taken up at its proper stage and there is enough opportunity for revision. The precaution to be observed is that the portion should neither be too long nor too short.

Presently "Topical Method" is more a system of arrangement of subject matter than a method of teaching. The topics is to be taught at a stretch, without a break or gap, continuous teaching of topic not only will save the students from divided attention and will also ensure their full and whole hearted concentration on the topic in hand. Thus, a natural link will exist in the day-to-day work in the class room.

Formation of Units

Units are formed to facilitate learning. Their function is to guide the student through a learning experience. Like most learning devices, the unit is a growth, an evolution, rather than a creation. The following points should be remembered while forming units:

1. Units for lower classes should be shorter than those meant for higher classes. So due consideration to class, grade and time be given while forming units.

2. Children's needs, interests, capacities and capabilities should always be kept in mind while selecting units for them. Thud, units should not be big enough to confuse children with factual material. They should, rather, centre round the children's expanding interests.

3. A unit must have relationship to the whole course.

4. A unit must be comprehensive enough on which sufficient material may be available for its complete understanding.

5. A good unit should provide for the intellectual, social and emotional development of children, through the integration and correlation of their learning activities.

6. A good unit should be evolutionary and functional, moving towards some definite goal.

7. Each unit should be further split up into sub-units for the sake of clarity. For example, the unit "How British Traders became Rulers of India" may be divided into the following sub-units:

(i) Early European settlements and emergence of the British as the leading power.

(ii) Decline of the Mughal Empire.

(iii) Rise and Fall of the Marathas.

(iv) Rise and Fall of Hyder Ali & Tippu.

(v) Rise and Fall of the Sikhs.

Procedure in Unit Plan

Dr. H.C. Morrison has set up a procedure that according to him will enable the pupils to accomplish the mastery of the unit. His procedure remains even today the most accepted. Like Harbartain steps, Morrison's procedure also consists of five formal steps which are under :

(i) Exploration. In this step, the teacher discovers what the pupils know about the proposed unit. This can be done by a formal written test or an informal class discussion. This step orients the teacher and motivates the pupils. It brings out the perceptive background of the pupils in the subject and prepares them for the new material.

(ii) Presentation. The teacher, presents to the class a complete outline of the unit through a short and well-planned talk. After the presentation, a test is given to find out whether the pupils have understood the idea of the unit. The talk is repeated for the second or even for the third time. If the teacher feels that the students have not understood the outline thoroughly.

(iii) Assimilation. This step needs the pupils to engage themselves in reading, studying, writing, talking with one another and consulting the teacher. They are guided by the teacher through study-sheets, containing references, assignments, projects, problems and other such material that teacher in view of teacher will help the pupils to achieve mastery of the unit.

(iv) Organisation. Each pupil is required to write a logical and systematic outline of the facts, he has gathered about that unit. It will demonstrate that he has understood the unit.

(v) Recitation. The pupils are now ready to recite and give a systematic oral account of all or of significant portions of the unit. This step is meant to afford training in speaking.

Importance of This Procedure

It becomes quite clear that in his procedure, Dr. Morrison has tried to utilize the best in modern educational theory and practice. The system may not be perfect, but "it does provide for individual differences remedial procedures, a scientific system of testing with follow-up work, the use of the sound method of supervised study under laboratory conditions, and to some extent, socialized procedure."

Advantages of Unit-Procedure

1. Gives a Variety of Outcomes. If the unit procedure is well-planned and skilfully executed, it gives a variety of outcomes. The extension of knowledge and the development of skills, abilities and attitudes are some of the possible outcomes. Many of the traits that history teachers wish to develop in their pupils, are especially promoted through the unit procedure. e.g. co-operation, courtesy, leadership, loyalty and respect for good workmanship, opportunities for reading, problem solving, project work, discussion and personal interviewing etc.

2. Provides a Natural Situation for Teaching Skills. If opportunities are not provided for development of skills, "the units become little more than chapters in books or logically organized segments of subject-matter." In order to enable children to learn how to work in groups, it is essential that group situations be provided. This is possible through the unit-procedure which provides such situations.

3. Provides Flexibility for Adapting Instruction to Individual Differences of Children. The unit procedure does not aim at fixed and uniform standard of achievement for all pupils. It rather focuses attention on the individual child, his problem and his interests. Well-planned units keep different standards of achievement in case of different children in order to meet the educational needs of individual pupils. This makes learning functional because units are based on the needs and interests of different types of children.

4. Effective use of Supplementary Materials. In the unit procedure pupils make use of text-books, source books, encyclopaedias, literature, pamphlets and periodicals etc. A well-planned unit stimulates the use of these and many other types of supplementary material.

5. Encourages Progressive Measures in Teaching-Learning

Process. In the educational field today, curriculum, correlation, fusion and integration are frequently mentioned. The unit method not only combines all these progressive measures but also encourages them.

6. Exemplifies Democracy in the Class-Room. The unit procedure exemplifies democracy as an ideal, in the best possible manner, in the class-room. Through this procedure, democracy is not only taught in spirit but can also be made the subject of the unit of study.

Limitations of this Procedure

Like any other method of teaching this method also has certain limitations which are as follow:

1. Insufficient Training in Unit Technique: At present history teachers have not sufficient training in the technique of forming units and putting them into execution. It may be due to the nature of teacher training programme in training institutions and because of the lack of sufficient text-books, periodicals, pamphlets and other supplementary materials.

2. Confusion on the Part of Pupils: If pupils are not taught by the unit procedure in all school subjects, they become confused when it is used only in one subject, namely, history. Such a lack of uniformity in teaching methods, leads to a general state of wonder, confusion and indecision.

3. Failure to Learn Certain Basic Facts: Many of the fundamental facts of history are never learned when this subject is taught through the unit plan. Specific characters dates, places and technical vocabulary are liable to be easily over-looked.

4. Unsympathetic Attitude of Visitors and Parents: If during the development of a unit, some visitors or parents happen to visit classes, they would often feel that the classwork is all confusion and without any substance. They do not understand that noise, accompanying actual work, is justified in this procedure.

REVISION QUESTIONS

1. Discuss the main characteristics of the Lecture Method of teaching History.

2. Discuss briefly the advantages and disadvantages of the Text-book Method of teaching History.
3. What is Story-telling method of teaching History ? How do you distinguish it from the Discussion Method ?
4. Differentiate between the Problem and the Project methods of teaching History.
5. What is the key-idea, underlying the Unit Method of teaching History. Discuss this method with all its merits.
6. What is the value of utilizing original sources in the teaching of History ? Mention the main difficulties in the way of following this method in our schools.
7. Name the different categories of sources that can be utilized with advantage, while teaching history in our schools.
8. Select one lesson for the 10th class which you would like to teach through the Source method. What steps would you follow for the successful utilization of the method ?
9. What is the Source Method of teaching History ? Indicate its advantages and disadvantages.
10. How would you use any one of the following methods in senior classes for increasing effective participation by your pupils:

    (i) Source Method, (ii) Project Method.

In your answer mention different activities that you will employ and the procedure of assessing the learning outcomes.

Chapter 6

Principles of History Teaching

6.1 INTRODUCTION

No subject is important in itself and its importance lies in presenting it before the students. If a subject is presented in a systematic and interesting manner by a teacher then he earns the reputation of a successful teacher. If presented in such a form that it is grasped by the students then students will be able to acquire a mastery over it. The presentation is always based on certain principles. In this respect Fenden has rightly observed, "the intellectual weakness of the child comes for the most part from his inability to fix his attention. His mind is like a lighted taper, in place exposed to the wind whose flame is ever shaky, therefore, it is the duty of a good teacher to serve and assist nature without forcing her in any way".

6.2 IMPORTANT POINTS IN TEACHING OF HISTORY

While teaching history, it is desirable for the teacher to keep following points in his mind.

(i) His entire attention remains focussed on the child.

(ii) He should be clear about the subject matter being taught.

(iii) He should use a proper teaching method for presenting the subject matter.

In history teaching there is no any one method that may be suitable for all topics and all levels. In the absence of it the teacher has to use his own judgment to select the most suitable method. Further history is an ever growing subject and every day now material is added to its subject matter. Thus teacher has to take extra pairs to collect teaching aids, he is required to use different teaching method at every different stage. This situation can be described, as under, in the words of an eminent scholar: "History perhaps beats over other subjects in the intensity of discussion and the heated argument that has centered round its teaching method in recent times.

6.3 GENERAL PRINCIPLES

In spite of all the changes that have taken place in the course of history, it cannot be denied that there are certain basic principles on which the teaching of history rests. Some general principles are as under:

(1) From Concrete to Abstract. While teaching history, the teacher should *proceed from concrete to abstract*. In the lower classes, concrete facts should be presented. With the growth in the mental age of the students, the teacher can resort to presentation of abstract facts. He should proceed from easy to complex, keeping in view the mental age of the students.

(2) From Known to Unknown. The *second maxim of the teaching* is that the teacher should proceed *from known to unknown*. The teacher tries to take advantage of what the students know and then tries to relate the new experiences with the old ones. In this process, the teacher should take reverse course. He should try to present the known facts to the students first and then take them to unknown areas.

(3) Chronological Order. To make subject intelligible to the students, *the facts should be presented in their chronological order*. This is all the more important in the teaching of history. Since history has a scientific outlook so it is necessary that the facts of history should be presented in a systematic and chronological manner.

(4) Co-relation of Facts and Events. Facts of history should not be presented independently and in an isolated manner. An attempt should be made to present various facts in a cor-related and co-ordinated manner with the events so that it may look like a chain of events. Every event and fact should be based on the 'Law of Cause and Effect'. Such a presentation is intelligible and understandable to the students.

(5) Pendulum Method. This method is useful at every stage of education. The pendulum moves backward and then forward. In other words, it establishes the connection of the past with the present. Similarly, the teacher of history should try to connect the past events and experiences with the present circumstances. If teacher succeeds in co-ordinating the past with the present, his teachings shall be interesting

and successful.

(6) Perfection. All the facts that are presented before the students should be perfect in themselves. It is not sufficient to present an outline only. All the events should be presented in their full form. This does not mean that the students should be burdened with informations only. They should be given only that much which is necessary. These events should be presented in a scientific manner and systematic order. An attempt should be made to shift the important from the unimportant and present what is actually needed.

(7) Aids. Teacher should make a balanced use of the teaching aids at every stage of education. Pictures, charts, maps, etc., are the life blood of the teaching of history. They make the history teaching effective and interesting. At no stage should the teacher try to discard these things.

(8) Mastery Over the Subject. The teacher should have perfect command over the topic that he is teaching. He should have prepared the lesson thoroughly well so that he may present it before the students is an interesting and attractive manner. On the other hand, the students should also be kept active. They should not be made passive partners in the game. Occasional question and dramatisation will do good.

(9) Keeping the Dry and Terse Matter Off. History has certain uninteresting and dry elements in it. Dates, names of rulers, places of events, etc., are not at all interesting to the students. The teacher should, therefore, try to make the subject interesting to the students and, if possible, do away with the unnecessary dates and names.

(10) Time Sense. At every stage of education, the students of history should be given time sense. Unless the students have developed a proper sense of time, it shall not be possible for them to co-ordinate and cor-relate knowledge of various subjects that they have acquired. In the absence of the 'Sense of Time', their knowledge shall be lopsided. It shall neither be completed nor systematized.

(11) Question and Answer. In the present methods of teaching, question and answer method is supposed to be good and interesting. The teacher should try to apply this method and make the teaching interesting. If the questions are put up to the students, they shall remain active and try to grasp the matter. The questions should be framed in an artistic manner. They should be framed that they awaken the curiosity

in the students and inspire them to come forward with the answer.

(12) Oral Teaching. In junior classes especially, oral teaching is very useful. At this stage, text-books are not very much needed. In this respect, a scholar has aptly remarked:

"In the junior stage especially, the oral lecture is the chief factor in presentation, as text-book is not essential. In the middle and senior secondary stages, there is definitely a need for the text-book because at this stage solid facts are given to the students."

REVISION QUESTIONS

1. Discuss the important points in teaching of history.
2. What are the main principles of history teaching ?
3. Discuss in detail the general principles of history teaching.

Chapter 7

Techniques of History Teaching

7.1 INTRODUCTION

In addition to methods of teaching, the History teachers make use of a variety of techniques for directing the learning processes. Techniques of teaching should serve the ends and objectives of the society. India is a democratic country and in this country the teaching of history be conducted on democratic lines. Prof. M.P. Muffut correctly states, "All techniques should be in line with democratic process and relate to the goods desired in the study of a topic. Techniques are employed for getting the learning underway with guidance from the teacher. They should be selected as a means of serving the best purpose of a particular time with the result of growth for the individual."

7.2 VARIOUS TECHNIQUES

The following are some of the techniques used by teachers of history:

i. Narration technique,

ii. Drill technique,

iii. Examination technique,

iv. Question answer technique,

v. Illustration technique,

vi. Dramatisation technique,

vii. Assignments,

viii. Review, and

ix. Supervised study.

These techniques are discussed at length in the following pages:

I. Narration Technique

In this technique, the teacher narrates the topic and the students try to acquire knowledge through the narration. This narration is made with an eye on the interest, objectives and attitudes of the pupils. Teacher makes an all out effort to present the subject-matter in a simple, interesting and intelligible way. Many a times this technique is adopted to supplement the question-answer technique.

The teacher must keep the following points in mind while using this technique.

(a) The narration should be in accordance with mental and physical age of the children.

(b) The narration should not be too lengthy.

(c) While using this technique the teacher should supplement it with question answer technique.

(d) An effort be made to make proper use of various teaching aids.

II. Drill Technique

It is the most widely used technique of teaching. It was originally introduced by *Thorndike*. It has become very popular among teachers because it can be used quite easily. This technique is based on the assumption that if a particular learning is revised several times, it becomes stable and permanent. Drill is not a mere repetition of an act for the purpose of attaining perfection, but it is a serious work activity for obtaining perfection, formation of habit or fixing of specific facts for easy and effortless recall, "**Drill**" is sometimes used as a synonym for "**Practice.**"

The Drill technique can be used only in some specific aspects in teaching of history. It is quite useful in learning the dates and names of events.

How to Make Drill Effective

To get best results the teacher should put in a lot of thinking while preparing the task. He should select and phrase questions which are brief and concise, on the unit or topic that has been studied. The teacher may try competitive exercise instead of asking questions in a straight forward manner. The contest is very appealing to the students but the real contest will depend upon teacher's planning.

Values of Effective Drill-work

(i) It aids in achieving complete mastery of the subject-matter.

(ii) It helps in isolating the most important points from those of lesser importance.

(iii) It helps in ascertaining the effectiveness of class-room work.

(iv) It helps pupils to prepare themselves for testing and evaluation.

(v) It increase employment by class-room work.

III. Examination Technique

In this technique, the teacher examines his students about the knowledge of the topics learnt by them. By this technique teacher can ascertain how far the students have assimilated the subject taught to them.

This method helps the teacher to ascertain how far he has been able to teach the lesson successfully.

While using this technique the teacher should keep the following points in mind:

(i) Only objective type tests be given and the questions asked should be short and to the point.

(ii) Teacher should remove the difficulties of the students.

(iii) Question be set in such a way that whole of the field of learning is covered.

(iv) While evaluating the test, teacher should remain impartial.

IV. Question-answer Technique

It is very important technique in the teaching of history. Through the use of this technique teacher makes an attempt to ascertain and evaluate the knowledge of his students about the subject. This technique is used to incite and awaken the curiosity in the students, and then using this curiosity and attempt is made to improve their knowledge.

In history this technique is useful for preparing unit plans, study guides and work sheets etc. For success of this technique it is essential that teacher knows the technique of formulating questions which stimulate and rouse the pupil's desire to learn.

Characteristics of Good Questions

(i) They should be such as can be easily and clearly understood.

(ii) They should be put in the simplest possible language.

(iii) Question should require specific answers and not general ones.

(iv) A good question should stimulate thinking on the part of all pupils, even though it may be addressed to only one of them.

(v) A good question is one that is definite and concise.

(vi) The question asked should be suited, in language and in the desired response, to the ability and maturity of the pupils.

While making use of this technique the teacher should bear the following points in mind:

(i) The questions be asked in a pleasant manner.

(ii) The question be stated first and then the students be called upon to answer it.

(iii) Questions should be distributed all over the class in such a way that the majority of students in the class take part in discussion.

(iv) Questions should not be asked very rapidly without giving sufficient time to pupils for thought.

(v) The needless repetition of questions should be avoided.

(vi) In handling the pupil's answers, the teachers must make every effort to be fair so that the pupils may feel free to respond and are encouraged rather than discouraged by the teacher's comments.

This technique is helpful in developing the power of expression of the students. This is also helpful in ascertaining their personal difficulties. On the basis of knowledge acquired an attempt may be made to remove the difficulties of the students.

V. Illustration Technique

While using this technique some illustrations are shown to the students so as to make the subject matter interesting and intelligible. The illustrations depicted should be scientific and should have a direct bearing on the content material. Various types of illustrations are in use e.g. maps, sketches, models, charts, graphs etc.

VI. Drama Technique

In this technique an attempt is made by the teacher to present different historical events in the form of a drama. He asks the students to enact scenes of history by dialogues and by wearing the dresses.

The use of this technique helps to keep active. Various sense organs of the students. It develops a creative element in the students and also helps in establishing a co-ordination between the head and the hand. It also removes the shyness of the students and so the technique is quite useful for the healthy growth of the personality of the child.

VII. Assignment

Assignment literally means "giving out of a task or job by a person in authority". However, as a technique of teaching assignment is a planning and organising period. In this period the teacher outlines tentatively the activities of the pupils in preparation for the study.

The modern approach to assignment stresses directed learning and co-operative planning. Each individual pupil or a group of pupil is given a task related to the topic under study and the students are expected to complete it with the help of work-books, text-books etc. For achieving progressive improvement proper guidance and direction are essential. All out efforts be made by the teacher to arouse pupil's interest in the assignments.

Characteristics of a Good Assignment

(i) It should be stated in clear and simple terms.

(ii) It should help to remove difficulties and main misunderstandings.

(iii) It should be stimulating and interesting.

(iv) It should recognise individual differences.

(v) It should be co-operative and must emphasise the "we" spirit.

(vi) It should be such as to develop insight and understanding amongst the students.

Importance of Assignments

Assignments provides proper guidance and direction to the activities of the pupils. It arouses their interest, provides motivation, prevents failures and prepares a sure ground for independent study. It is also helpful to the teacher as it helps him to improve his technique of teaching.

Evaluation of Assignment

To evaluate an assignment is a must to find if the students have shown any progress in their study periods and have shown more interest in the subject of history. No doubt, it is not possible to measure the definite effectiveness of an assignment but it can be made to certain extent making use of good check lists. Evaluation hare is concerned not only with academic achievements of students but is also concerned with their development in terms of desirable behaviour changes in relation to their feelings, thinking and actions. It is in this broader conception of evaluation that we should measure the effectiveness of the assignments technique.

VIII. Review

It is used to master those facts and skills which are considered very essential both in school and life. It consists of a recall of facts for the purpose of renewing those facts with a view to attain a mastery over them.

Review is different from drill in that it is a new view of previously learned facts and skills and not a mere repetition of them. It is a reorganisation of material from a different point of view. The review is a more broader and more inclusive term than drill.

Importance of Review in History

(i) All the modern procedures of teaching make good use of this technique, e.g., it is used in Dalton laboratory plan. The problem, the project and the unit methods of teaching.

(ii) It stimulates pupils interest in activity.

(iii) It helps in understanding the cause and effect relationships.

IX. Supervised Study

It is an important technique for teaching of history. This implies "Supervision of the teacher or a group of class of pupils, as they work at their desks or around their tables". While supervising his students the teacher is available to his students whenever they find any difficulty. He is always ready to help and assist them when asked to do so.

"Supervised study is the effective direction and over-sight of the silent study and laboratory activities of the pupils."

Pupil's silent study may consist of reading, interpreting or writing activities and laboratory work. It may involve the collection or selection of reference material, preparation of illustrative aids, debates, discussions etc. It is thus clear that "supervised study is an activity period in which both teacher and the pupils work together to accomplish desirable goals." A supervised study can make the teacher to note various deficiencies of his pupils and he can then plan to make them up. Now educationists are of the firm opinion that school is the only place where a pupil can do much more work in a better way and lesser time. However, the work to be done under the supervision of a teacher must be interesting and enjoyable for the pupil.

Plans of Supervised Study

The following plans are formed to be more helpful.

(i) The Conference Plan: Under this plan the teacher remains in the class-room for another extra period and provides individual help to such students who lag behind in their studies. It is quite helpful for weak students to make up their deficiencies.

(ii) The Special Teacher Plan: The special teacher appointed to help students must be very kind hearted, sympathetic and should possess a wide knowledge of many subjects. He must also have a sound knowledge of child psychology.

(iii) The Study Hall Plan: A room set apart for supervised study is referred to as *Study Hall*. The students work in Study Hall and may get help from other pupils or from the teacher in case of difficulties. However, perfect discipline has to be maintained in the Study Hall.

For the purpose of class recitation, the following types of plans are used.

(i) The Divided-Period Plan. In this plan the class-period time is divided between the usual class recitation and the supervised study. For this division the teacher provides the necessary direction and guidance. With such an arrangement students get ample opportunities for

independent study under the direct supervision of the class-teacher.

(ii) The Double-Period Plan. It is quite similar to divided-period plan except that two complete periods are set apart for his purpose instead of one.

(iii) The Fixed Study-Period Plan. A number of head-masters recommend a fixed period for supervised study. It may be extra period added to school time-table or one hour a week for supervised study in each subject.

Advantages of Supervised Study

(i) It meets individual differences.

(ii) The teacher can detect the slow workers and can guide them into effective learning experiences, which are meaningful to them.

(iii) It promotes better pupil-teacher relationship.

(iv) It develops the senses of belongingness and achievement.

(v) By this plan a more efficient use of sources and materials becomes possible.

(vi) It helps in developing certain important skills, e.g., age of maps, charts, atlases etc.

Limitations of Supervised Study

(i) It does not help bright students.

(ii) It destroys self-reliance on the part of the pupils.

Supervised study plan will, however, depend upon circumstances. But whenever it is possible, the history teacher must utilize this important technique of directing his pupils learning.

REVISION QUESTIONS

1. What is Supervised Study technique ? What purpose does it serve in History ?
2. List the values of Supervised Study in history.
3. Discuss the various plans of Supervised Study.
4. How can the reading programme in history be improved through

Supervised Study ?

5. Discuss the limitations of Supervised Study Technique.

6. Name the different techniques which a history teacher should employ with different age groups, during the course of teaching.

7. Why should we emphasise the need for effective assignment technique?

8. What are the essential characteristics of a good assignment ?

9. Why should assignment grow out of the activities and interests of pupils ?

10. Enumerate the characteristics of good questions.

11. How can we make use of questioning technique in history in an effective manner ?

12. How should a teacher deal with pupil's questions ?

13. What are the chief outcomes of questioning ?

14. Discuss the importance of drill as a technique of history instruction.

15. How does the review differ from drill ?

16. Mention the various review activities for a history class.

17. What are the purposes involved in the use of notebooks by history teachers ?

18. Discuss the most important advantages and disadvantages of the use of work-books.

19. How does a work-book differ from notebook ? What should a work-book contain ?

Chapter 8

Curriculum of History

8.1 INTRODUCTION

History occupies an important place in the school curriculum. Till about 20-30 years back history was taught as one subject history and geography under the head general knowledge. Now we have realised the importance of teaching history and it occupies an honourable place in school curriculum in its own right.

The construction of curriculum of history is a difficult task, however, it would be easier to construct a syllabi in history if we keep certain points in mind, while constructing the curriculum in history.

The syllabus of mainly bound by two considerations.

(i) Structure of the subject, and

(ii) Limited and maturing abilities of the pupils.

The structure of the subject, in most cases, requires that a wide range of elementary rules and techniques be mastered before studying the rest of the subject.

The consideration of limited and maturing abilities of students decides the order in which the contents of the subject are to be arranged.

In case of history it is not essential to master foundation elements before acquiring any real knowledge or skill. However, since the field of study is too wide and the quantity of historical material is enormous and so there is the actual problem of selection in this case.

8.2 PROBLEMS OF SELECTION

This problems arises because knowledge cannot be imparted to the pupils within the short span of their school life. Thus the actual problem is to compress so many facts and details in history syllabus. In our country, in the pre-independence days, the history syllabus suffered from the defect of poor selection and deficient grading. The same facts were repeated in different grades putting under emphasis on political "outlines" to the total neglect of social and cultural life.

From this we may conclude that a ruthless selection of relevant facts should be our guiding principle in syllabus construction. Here we face a problem of selection of events and the problem of their historical explanation. Take for example the Events of 1857. For Britishers, it was simply a mutiny of the soldiers but the Indians claim it to be the first war of Independence.

Again there is the problem of "selection of periods", i.e., which particular periods of history are more worthy of study than other?

Another problem is releted to the "Aspect history", i.e., are some aspects of history more important than others ?

Another problem of selection relates to the conflicting claims of world history and the history of a country. Are we free to choose between them ? Or, has the history of the particular country any special claims to be taught ?

In view of the above noted problems we have to make a fair selection of materials. While doing so, we should take note of the various forces, spiritual, material, the great religious, the achievements of science, the arts, vast range of social customs, family life, festivals, amusements, great deeds of heroism and kindness and love.

We shall first of all study the contributions made by the cultural. Epoch theory and then Biographical theory and finally Psychological theory or Spiral theory.

8.3 CULTURAL EPOCH THEORY

This theory was one of the earliest attempts of frame history syllabus on psychological foundations. It held away in the educational world during nineteenth century. Its major implication is that the "childhood of history is best for the child, the boyhood of history for the boy, the youthhood of history for the youth and manhood of history for the man."[1]

1. Johnson, H., *Teaching of History*, New York, The Macmillan Company, 1940, p. 93.

Its basic idea is that ancient history is suitable for elementary stages, mediaeval history for the middle stage and modern history for the high school stage.

The importance of this theory lies in the fact that it lays more stress on social and economic events and problems pertaining to humanity. According to this theory, the student shall know about the various stages of development of the culture of human race, and when they have finished their education, they shall be having full idea of the development of human civilisation.

Critics of the theory point out that human progress did not occur in an orderly way. The progress at every stage was not at all systematic. Human society did not come down like a flight of stars. There were various turns and ups and downs in the path of progress of human race. Unless we have an idea of all these things, we shall not be able to have an idea of the development of human race.

It cannot be said that the last stage of the development of human race is most complex. In the modern history, the language is easy as compared to the language of ancient history. If the curriculum is organised on the basis of this, it shall be difficult to arrange various military events. In the ancient history, political and military events are most important and it is not possible to have an idea of the history without knowing these things thoroughly well.

8.4 BIOGRAPHICAL THEORY

This theory has influenced the selection of materials, at least, for the elementary stage. It is claimed that general history is beyond the comprehension of the children below 12 or 13. Therefore, they should be introduced to great men of our country and of the world in a strictly chronological sequence. This idea originated in the great man theory of historical explanation propounded by Carlyle. He believed, "The history of what man has accomplished in this world is at bottom the history of the great men who have worked here".

The advocates of this theory think that great men represent their times. They are the noblest creation of God. So the preliminary study of their lives will equip the student to have an insight into the history. Their biographies will form the basis for further study of movements at a later stage.

Criticism of the Theory

The critics of this theory point out that it does not recognise the collective life of the community. It also does not take into account the role to collective social endeavour. Instead, it harps on the personality of the great heroes and advocates hero-worship. Actually, the so-called great men do not represent their time. They are far above the average humanity of their age. They do not symbolize the various aspects of the life of the community.

Whatever the critics may point out, the theory has greatly influenced teaching in schools and has supplied suitable material for the beginners. Even Pt. Nehru was highly impressed by the value of biographies. He pertinently remarked, "I cannot remove from the gallery of my mind the pictures of persons and events which I hung there is my boyhood and youth. These pictures have coloured my outlook on history".

The value of the approach lies in the selection of right personalities. Not only the great men and women of our own country but great personalities from different parts of world should find a place in the syllabus. Along with the heroes, warriors, statesmen who have shaped the destiny of our nation, men of science, explores, inventors, fighters for freedom, leaders of peace, men of letters, artists and a host of others should be included in the history syllabus.

8.5 PSYCHOLOGICAL THEORY OR SPIRAL THEORY

The main aim of this theory is to meet the psychological needs and requirements of the children. The subject-matter of the history should be so selected and organised that the students may find satisfaction in fulfilment of their mental needs.

According to this theory, subject-matter of the history at the *elementary stage or the primary stage*, should be concrete. Abstract material shall be difficult for the students of this stage of education. They should be acquainted with the various elements of history through local history. Past experiences and the lives of great men may be presented before them in a systematic and orderly manner. It has rightly been remarked in this connection:

The earliest stage being presented in nature, history will be made as concrete as possible.

Then comes the *next stage*. The subject matter of history at this stage of education, should be so organised that it may lead to the development of the power of imagination. The students should also be trained to keep the historical facts in their mind. The following quotation presents this well:

History of the representative type will be planned at the disposal of the child in the second stage, in accordance with his representative period which characterised by retention of facts and strong imagination.

Then we reach the third stage. At this stage, such events should be presented before the students that may make them to understand their meanings. In this regard the following quotation is worth mentioning:

This theory of history which aims at giving deeper understanding of the movements that were taught at the earlier stages in developing cause and effect, sequence of facts and which help pupils to draw inferences and verify conclusions, will be taught in the third stage of child's development.

For selecting the subject matter of history, the views of Prof. Ghat are very important. He has laid it down in the following works:

(i) Select one central idea or a group of associated ideas to build up the structure round it at junior stage.

(ii) Select facts which will bear interpretation and will fit in with a scheme of human development of progress.

(iii) Select facts which will provide continuity and unity in their treatment of history in chronological order.

(iv) Select facts which well, in one way or the other, explain the present day world.

8.6 PRINCIPLES OF SYLLABUS CONSTRUCTION

The following are the broad principles that should be observed while making a selection of historical facts.

(i) The syllabus must meet the aims and objectives of teaching history.

(ii) The syllabus should be based on the present needs, requirements and the circumstances of the child. The child needs experiences more than instructions, i.e., the syllabus should be child oriented.

(iii) The syllabus should be community centred. Since the child is to be educated thorough the society in which he is born so the good of individual and good of society cannot be separated.

(iv) The syllabus should be based on the principle of integration. It means that the activities carried on in a school, should not be treated in water-tight compartments, but should be so conducted as to lead the whole child to a functional unity with the environment.

(v) The syllabus be framed on the principle of flexibility.

(vi) While framing the syllabus forward-looking principle should be kept in mind.

(vii) It should be broad based.

(viii) It should present an over all, balanced plan for growth in human relationship.

(ix) It should be tentative rather than final.

8.7 CONTENTS OF THE HISTORY SYLLABUS

Here we give some positive and practicable suggestions about the contents of the history syllabus. Here these will be stated only in general terms without making any attempt to detail them for any particular age group.

If we look at the history syllabus being following in different countries, we find that these have been desired to meet the requirements of their own national outlook. In our own country we want to develop in our children a sense of appreciation of our cultural heritage and also to faster in them a world outlook. A balance has to be made between these two, i.e., the claims of our own society and the claim of world community. The history syllabus in our schools should, therefore, be selected from the following fields:

(i) Early History. It includes the history of man in stone age.

(ii) World History. It is essential to understand the contributions of different people to the development of human society. It includes

the story of ancient civilisation, the origin and growth of great religions, life of middle ages, Renaissance and Reformation etc.

(iii) National History. It should form the core of our history syllabus. To that core, the history of other peoples and civilisations must be organically related.

(iv) Local History. It should form an important part of syllabus in history for the beginners.

(v) Social, Economical and Cultural History. Topics selected for social economic and cultural history will supplement the pupil's study in political history. Their emphasis on interdependence of people will generate a feeling of universal brotherhood among the pupils, so vitally essential for creating a world understanding.

8.8 ORGANISATION OF SUBJECT-MATTER IN HISTORY

Selection is subject-matter is not enough it has to be organised in some proper way. Without proper organisation the purpose will not be achieved. An effort be made to present the subject-matter, before the children, in such a way that they feel interested in the study of history. For this purpose the following plans and theories act as guides.

1. The Concrete System of Plan

In this system the child is first acquainted with those things that are already known to him. Such things that have a bearing on creative activities of the child. Afterwards the subject-matter be made more comprehensive and organised in accordance with the age and mental capacity of the child. This plan is based on the principle of *whole to part.* In it the teacher proceeds from *simple to complex.*

The main criticism against this theory is that it lays too much stress and repeated references to the events, creates impediments in the natural flow of interest of children. This aspect of theory is highlighted by the following quotation:

To develop the time sense of the pupils as the distance in time between events and characters will not be properly grasped by the pupils owing to the history of some two thousand years being covered in a short time.

2. Periodic Method

In this method we divide the history into various periods and then these are studied in chronological order. It has been remarked that *chronology is the essential skeleton of history* and so the whole skeleton is studied in various parts of these periods.

Johnson says, "History for schools had begun as a chronological survey, and when it become a continuous study from year to year of school course, it remained a chronological survey".[2]

In this method the ground once covered is never repeated. The whole course is divided into several well-marked stages. In the pre-independence days. Indian history was divided into Hindu period, Muslim period, British period etc.

Its supports recommend this method on the following grounds:

1. It utilises the natural order of events and thereby enables the pupils to grasp the idea of 'time factor' in history. They can witness the long array of events on the canvass of succeeding generations and in the process, develop a chronological outlook.

2. Another advantage is that during the successive years of school instruction, students are introduced to new periods—periods efflorescent with new problems—and so their interest in the subject is sustained. Every time a fresh ground is covered and, therefore, there is no room for dullness and monotony to set in the process of instruction.

3. Moreover, the syllabus formed on chronological lines accords most naturally with the way in which history itself has developed.

Limitations. There are certain defects in this theory as well. They are being enumerated below :

(a) It is wrong to say that by this method, we become acquainted with the various stages of the development of the mind.

(b) Events of the ancient history are so difficult and complicated that it is difficult for the students of tender age to follow them.

(c) If the teacher of history is not efficient, and does not prefer to repeat the various facts already taught by him, then the students will

2. Johnson Henry, *Teaching of History*, New York, Macmillon and Company, 1940 p. 89.

find it difficult to remember what they have learnt in the past.

(d) Those students, who leave the studies in between, do not have any idea about all events of history. Their knowledge of history remains incomplete.

Besides, there are other objections:

1. The critics of the chronological method point out that there is "no principle of selection except that of the order of occurrence of events. There are no themes around which facts are grouped".[3]

2. In such a treatment as Professor Jeffreys pertinently remarks, "it is difficult to give the pupil a sense of purpose or direction. He is not working for anything except for the end of the chapter".[4]

3. A syllabus based on the chronological order of presentation, remarks Burston, "would only meet pedagogical criteria if the remote periods were simple and elementary, and if history gradually became more difficult as it became more recent. Some might maintain that this was so, but most would argue that all periods have aspects which are too difficult for junior forms and so a chronological syllabus is only possible at the cost of study of some difficult aspects in the early periods".[5]

4. It allows the development of human history and not the child's mind to determine the outline at least, what history is taught to pupils at particular age levels.[6]

5. It involves the learning of dates and ultimately forges into drudgery.

3. Topical Method

In this method the subject matter of history is divided into various topics. It facilitates class-room teaching. This method was introduced by comenius to overcome the difficulties inherent in chronological method.

While dividing the syllabus into topics we should keep in mind that the whole subject may not be taught in isolation. As remarked

3. Vajreshwari, R.. A *Handbook for History Teachers*, Allied Publishers, p. 161.
4. Jeffevs, M.V.C., *History in Schools*. Landon, Pitman, 1939, p. 32.
5. Burston W.H., *Principles of History Teaching*, Macmillan and Co. Ltd. 1963, pp. 110-111.
6. IAAM, *The Teaching of History*, C.U.B., 1952, p. 20.

by an eminent scholar, "A topic should not be an isolated incident or episode but should present a factor which influence the main current of history".

According to Prof. Walsh, each topic contains several events, but they are logically and intelligently inter-related as being part of the same movement or policy.

Merits

(i) This method provides a solution for dealing with vast historical material.

(ii) It can be adopted according to the age, ability and aptitude of the children. This flexibility is significant in case of projects such as about transport, trade, houses etc.

(iii) Study of history through this method imparts a sense of purpose to the pupils.

(iv) It enables the teacher to control the subject matter and adapt it to the varying needs of the children.

Demerits

(i) It lays more emphasis on social aspect of history at the cost of other aspects of human life.

(ii) In it emphasis is laid on past and present and the past is supposed to provide a background for the development of present institutions and ideas.

4. Regressive Method

In this method of teaching history we move from present to the past. This is based on the theory that past should be studied as an explanation of the present. We give below an opinion about this method:

> *The teacher chooses certain vital, social or economical problems of today as a starting point or introduction, goes back to the remote past which has laid this problem or the state of things, again comes back to the period that immediately concerns him and follows the chronological order. Thus, the teacher regresses to come forward again. This plan is based on the mechanism 'go from the known to the unknown'.*

Merits

(i) Teaching by this method, we can establish in the mind of the students an essential relationship between the past and the present.

(ii) It inculcates in students an interest in the history of the present.

(iii) It helps in liberalising the attitude of the children and their activity is enlisted almost at every point.

Limitations

(i) It lays too much emphasis on the events and problems of present and their background in past and neglects the future.

(ii) It reverses the chronological order.

(iii) It is unpsychological.

(iv) It is burdensome for the students.

5. The 'Patch' Method

The method which has become quite popular in modern times was given by Miss Majorie Reeves. In this method the teacher does not make any attempt to make his pupils acquire in the school any detailed chronological outline of knowledge, nor does he ask them to go over the same course again and again in successive grades. He also does not proceed by topics. Instead he chooses short but significant epochs in man's history such as 'India in the Sixth century B.C.', 'the Gupta period, 'the Elizabethan age' and uses these as the basis of study. The idea is to allow the pupils to "soak themselves in the atmosphere of these periods, finding out of how people lived and earned their living, how they fed themselves, what they wore, what their amusements were, what they believed in, what sort of government they had, and so on.[7]

Merits

(1) The advocates of this system claim that the value of historical study in school lies precisely in the process of 'getting under the skin' of a particular age and this system provides opportunity to delve deeply.

(2) Another value claimed for the patch system is that its study gives "practice in that most salutary art, the art of entering into an entirely

7. Burston and Green, *Handbook for History Teachers*, Methuen & Co., 1962, p. 8.

different atmosphere and point of view of one's own", because the patch being studied, may have no obvious or continuous connection with any present day institutions of pre-conceptions.[8]

Demerits

Despite the above advantages claimed, the opponents of the system point out that it does not provide a comprehensive system of grading historical material. It is bound to leave great gaps in their knowledge and give them a confused picture of chronology.

8.9 CONTENT OF HISTORY AT DIFFERENT STAGES OF EDUCATION

I. Content of History at Primary Stage

At the primary stage the history be closely related to the abilities and characteristics of the age of children. The work should start with the realities which are near to the children in space and time. They be introduced to *local traditions*, the problems faced by their fore-fathers etc.

They should also be given a glimpse of the life of the earliest man. At this stage children should also be made aware of the contributions of great men in different fields of life. To achieve it the syllabus should have stories about heroes of war and prophets of peace, men of letters and pioneers of science, saints and sages, artists and patriots etc.

Children should also be given a glimpse into the social conditions and elements of daily social life of ancient times. It will remind them of the value of daily work of ordinary people and will make them aware of the change in the order of things with the progress of time.

II. Content of History at Secondary Stage

The content of history at this stage of education, as suggested by C.P. Hill, should consist of *national history* with special emphasis on those topics which help to an understanding of present day problems or which enable the students to note the differences the similarities between life in earlier times and life today.

8. *Teaching History*, Pamphlet No 23 HMSO, p. 18.

In addition to national history some topics about the history of the countries, geographically contiguous and culturally related should also be included in syllabus.

C.P. Hill says, "National history should always be taught against international background...Developments at home should be related to external events... the cultural relationships between different nations and areas should be made clear...There should be frequent comparisons of social change..."[9] There are teachers who prefer one independent outline course in world history at this stage. A group of others may like to introduce topics or problems such as the development of government and history of religions, the story of tolerance, the ideas of liberty and law while a different kind of proposal comes from third group of teachers. They want in addition to learning their own national history pupils should study in some detail the history of nations and regions which are dissimilar to their own land. Thus as C.P. Hill suggests we can weave around the core of national history, the fabric of social history, religious history, man's struggle for toleration and peace international co-operation, etc.

III. History Syllabus as Recommended by Ministry of Education

The Ministry of Education, Government of India, has published the contents of history in Indian schools for grades one to eleven. A brief enumeration of these contents will not be out of place here.

Class I. The students should be introduced to the following facts at this stage:

(1) *Local Traditions*—stories relating to local social workers saints religious places, historical places, local fairs, etc.

(2) *Stories of the ancient man*—stories about food, utensils, tools, ways of living of the cave man and the people of stone age and the copper age.

(3) *Practical work*— (a) visit to local places like museums, etc., and (b) making clay models of historical untensils, toys and tools.

Class II. At this stage local traditions and stories about ancient culture should be included in the syllabus. For example—a broad

9. Hill, C.P., *Op. Cit*, p. 74.

view of the local traditions taught in class I; stories about Babylon, Mohenjo-Daro, Arkpolis, Pyramids, etc.; life of the pupils in Ashramas and its comparison with Chinese, Greek and Roman life.

Practical work. As in the first grade. Besides, preparation of models, coins of clay and album of historical pictures should be done at this age.

Class III. Stories for ancient India, for example, Rama, Krishna, Buddha, Mahabir, Alexander, Ashoka, Kanishka, Chandragupta, Vikramaditya etc. These stories are to be presented in a chronological order.

Practical work—Pupils should be helped to understand distance and direction and initiated in map-drawing. They should be taught how to make an album of historical pictures, dramatise events and do craft work.

Class IV. Stories from medieval India, e.g., Prophet Muhammad, Muslim invasions on India, Prithviraj, All-ud din Khilji, Feroz Tuglaq, Chaitanya, Nanak, Kabir, Krishna, Deo Rai, Akbar, Chandbibi, Maharana Pratap, Aurangzeb, Shivaji, Nadir Shah, Baji Rao I and Baji Rao II, etc.

Practical work. As in class III, children's albums should contain pictures of art and architecture of the Mughal period.

Class V. Stories from modern India; Clive, Mir Kasim, Tipu Sultan, Nana Fadnavis, Ranjit Singh, Jhansi Ki Rani, Martyrs of First War of Independence, Raja Ram Mohan Roy, Syed Ahmed Khan, Vivekanand, Annie Besant, Pheroze Shah Mehta, Surendra Nath Banerjee, Motilal Nehru, Mahatma Gandhi, Subhash Chander Bose, Jawahar Lal Nehru, Sardar Patel, etc.

Practical work. As in above grades.

Class VI. Evolution of Indian society from ancient period to the Sultanate with emphasis on economic, social, religious and political aspects. The following topics may be included.

(1) Sources of Indian History;

(2) Indus Valley Civilisation;

(3) Aryan Civilisation;

(4) Epic Age;

(5) Jainism & Buddhism;
(6) Alexander's invasion, the Nandas, the Mauryas;
(7) Maurya—Sythian Civilisation;
(8) Kushan empire;
(9) Gupta empire:—Gupta period—why a golden age ?
(10) Invasion of the Huns;
(11) History of South India;
(12) Colonial and cultural expansion;
(13) Rise of Islam;
(14) The slave dynasty;
(15) The Khilji dynasty:
(16) The Tughlaq dynasty;
(17) Bahmani and Vijai Nagar Kingdoms;
(18) The Syed dynasty;
(19) The Lodi dynasty; and
(20) Culture of the Sultanate period and its impact on Indian life.

Practical work. Drawing of time-lines, historical maps, charts. sketches; dramatisation; tour of historical places and visit to museums, Preparation of clay models.

Class VII. Development of Indian Society from the Mughal period to the Company rule.

Topics:

(1) Invasions of Babur and establishment of Mughal empire;
(2) Humayun & Sher Shah;
(3) Akbar;
(4) Jehangir and Shah Jehan;
(5) Shah Jehan's reign—way a golden age ?
(6) Aurangzed and his policy;
(7) Rise of the Marathas;
(8) Coming of the Europeans;
(9) Expansion of British power;
(10) Rise of the Sikhs;
(11) The East India Company—power struggle;

(12) First War of Independence;

(13) Cultural history of the Mughal period; and

(14) State of culture, educational, religious and social reforms during the East India Company's rule.

Practical work. As in Class VI.

Class VIII. Modern India. The following topics should be included.

(1) Constitutional history;

(2) Development of Indian Administration;

(3) History of freedom struggle;

(4) History of education;

(5) History of Local-self Government;

(6) Economic history;

(7) New India—(history of Post-Independence era.); and

(8) Indian Constitution.

Practical Work— As in the above grades.

Classes IX, X, XI

(1) Critical study of Indian history;

(2) World history, and

(3) Important movements in the west;

(a) Renaissance and Reformation;

(b) French Revolution;

(c) Nationalism in Europe;

(d) Industrial Revolution;

(e) Rise of Socialism;

(f) International organisation—the League of Nations and the U.N.O.

(g) Development of Science.

(4) History of Eastern and South Eastern countries;

(a) China;

(b) Afghanistan;

(c) Japan;

(d) Indonesia;

(e) Burma and Tibet.

(5) Present problems in India;

(a) History of the progress of science in India;

(b) History of Indian agriculture and its problems;

(c) Industrial Problems;

(d) Language Problem;

(e) Social Problems;

(f) Economic Problems;

(g) Problems of Education.

Practical Work.

(a) Drawing of maps;

(b) Use of sources;

(c) Use of newspapers;

(d) Use of historical journals, magazines and papers;

(e) Tour of historical places;

(f) Collection of coins and historical albums;

(g) Drawing of time charts, sketches, and pictorial graphs, etc.

8.10 PRESENTATION OF SUBJECT MATTER OF HISTORY

After we have selected the subject, matter and have arranged it in proper order the next question that arises is of persecuting it before students, Teacher can use any one or methods of presentation in accordance with the age of students and their class. The following fundamentals should, however, be always kept in mind while presenting the subject-matter before the students.

(1) In the classroom, the teacher should try to present fact in a simple, intelligible and effective manner. Preciseness always pays.

(2) There is very little scope for discussion and presentation of the differences of opinion in the lower classes. It may be useful in higher classes.

(3) The teacher should invariably proceed from 'simple to complex' and 'concrete to abstract'. He should try to localise the subject-matter with the help of maps and charts etc.

(4) The time sense of the students should be developed by and by. In the beginning, the students should be acquainted with the events of

the present and then an attempt should be made to take them back to the past.

(5) The law of cause and effect must be utilised in teaching at every stage of education.

(6) An attempt should be made to correlate the present experiences with the past.

(7) While teaching history, effect should be made to throw light on the various aspects of the history. Unnecessary and irrelevant materials should be discarded.

(8) Dramatization and other activity methods make history interesting and real.

(9) The facts should be treated fully at the time of presentation.

I. Presentation of Subject-matter or History at Primary Stage of Education

This stage of education runs up to fifth class where children between the age group of 6-11 years come for study. This is the stage when children are very fond of listening to stories. These stories may deal with any part of the world or any part of the life.

The teacher of history should try to present the subject-matter in the form of stories. These stories should encourage the activities of the children. The stories should also be told in an interesting manner.

In order to be a successful story-teller, the teacher should have perfect command over the subject-matter. He should also be well aware of the psychology of the students.

The stories should be so arranged that they may continue to awaken the curiosity of the students, to know things by saying and doing, and also get on with the historical materials.

It is also recommended that teacher, at this stage of education, should use to the maximum possible extent various teaching aids such as pictures, charts, models, maps etc. He should also put special attention to the use of black-board, text-books etc.

II. Presentation of the Subject-mater of History at the Junior Stage of Education

The teaching of history at this stage of education should be organised on the psychological principles as enumerated below:

(1) Stress can be laid on the element of characterisation in the subject-matter.

(2) The facts should be properly explained before the students. An attempt may be made to assess their value in the light of the problems of the present-day.

(3) Time sense should be developed further.

At this stage the teacher should try to present facts and events of history in a systematic and chronological order but is an interesting way: He should keep in mind the maxim of "proceeding from concrete to abstract." An attempt should also be made by the teacher to correlate the events of history with problems of society as they exist-to-day.

At the stage of education the text-books be used to a larger extent and the black-board shall be used quite often. An outline of the subject matter may be put up on the black-board and the students be asked to develop these outlines at home. The students should also be given home-task and asked to do written work. In addition to the use of maps and charts, the students may be asked to dramatise and enact the various scenes of history. Teacher can ask the students to draw maps and may be asked to fill in the places of historical importance in maps. These things may also be given as home-task.

III. Presentation of the subject-matter of the History at the Secondary Stage of Education

At this stage of education the teaching should be so organised that it may meet the requirements of adolescence. At this stage of education the teacher should try to present certain problems and encourage the students to solve them. The text-books and black-board be used freely at this stage. Sketches may be drawn on the black-board and the subject-matter may be explained with the help of these sketches class-room discussion can be arranged to discuss certain topics and places of historical importance. Students be encouraged to do written work and for this they may be given home-work. The teacher should check, the home-work and give his suggestions to improve their working. He should ask the students to organise voluntary bodies so as to encourage the teaching of history. The history at this stage be taught in the background of word history. Pupils at this stage be encouraged to read newspapers and extra-books. Source books, if available, are really useful.

REVISION QUESTIONS

1. Briefly describe the importance of various methods of grading history.
2. What are the merits and limitations of chronological method of organising facts ?
3. Explain 'Concentric method' and compare it with 'Regressive method' of organising history syllabus.
4. Write short notes on :

   (a) Patch system,

   (b) Topical method.

Chapter 9

Teaching Aids in History

9.1 INTRODUCTION

The most difficult problem before a history teacher is to invest pupils to gain an experience of human behaviour in past societies. Through verbal expositions, be this to explain the past happenings but their time appreciation demands that events of past are understood in their casual and sequential relationships. In this respect audiovisual aids, with their various devices, techniques and resources, come to the help of the history teacher.

Audiovisual aids are the effective tools that "invest the past with an air of reality." Teaching aids should be used to supplement the process of teaching. Teaching aids make teaching concrete, effective and interesting. By making an appeal to the auditory and visual senses of pupils, audiovisual aids invest reality to the past, increase pupil's interest in the subject and supplement verbal explanations of the teacher.

"Any device which by sight or sound increases the individual's experience, beyond that acquired through reading may be described as an audiovisual aid to learning."

9.2 IMPORTANCE OF TEACHING AIDS

(i) They make the lesson of history interesting.

(ii) They help to stabilize the knowledge of the subject.

(iii) They make the process of learning interesting and practical.

(iv) They help the teacher to proceed 'from concrete to abstract'.

(v) They help the teacher to conduct the teaching efficiently and creditably.

(vi) They are a good substitutes for direct experiences and are a supplement to direct experience.

(vii) They are very helpful for poor readers and slow-learners.

(viii) They help to develop the power of imagination and observation.

(ix) They provide an opportunity for a change in the monotonous atmosphere that generally prevails in the class-room.

(x) They provide an opportunity for a better rapport between the teacher and his pupil.

(xi) They help the pupil to develop a scientific attitude.

(xii) They provide a training in scientific method.

(xiii) They can be used in bigger classes.

(xiv) Use of such aids is based on the principles of psychology.

9.3 PRINCIPLES FOR USE OF TEACHING AIDS

Following points are important for use of teaching aids:

(i) They should be woven with class-room teaching and should be used only to supplement the oral and written work being done in the class.

(ii) An effort be made that the teaching aids used in class are in conformity with the intellectual level of the students as is in accordance with the previous experience of the students.

(iii) Only such aids be preferred which provide a stimulus to the students for greater thinking and activity.

(iv) They should be exact, accurate and real as far as possible.

(v) The teacher should use a teaching aid only when he is quite sure about handling a specific teaching aid.

(vi) The teacher should use a teaching aid only after proper planning so that the aid is used exactly at the point, in the process of teaching, when it best fits in the process of teaching.

(vii) Teacher should see that a follow up programme follows the lesson in which a teaching aid has been used.

(viii) Teacher should carry out occasional evaluation about the use, function and effect of a teaching aid on the learning process.

9.4 TYPES OF TEACHING AIDS

For convenience of discussion the teaching aids in history may be grouped as under:

(i) Traditional aids, e.g., Text-books, black-board etc.

(ii) Visual aids, e.g., charts, pictures, graphs, maps and globe, stereoscopes, motion pictures, specimens and models.

(iii) Auditory aids, e.g., Radio, dictaphone, Loud speaker, phonograph, gramophone etc.

(iv) Audiovisual aids, e.g., Television, Sound-Motion pictures, Dramatisation, Field trips and school journeys.

A few of these aids will be discussed in detail.

1. Text-books

For various classes text-books are prescribed. They contain the subject-matter prescribed for a class but these books should not be used as reading-books in the class. They should help the students to prepare the lesson at home.

Qualities and Characteristics of the Text-books

The chief qualities and characteristics of the text-books are as follows:

(1) Description of the historical events should be presented in the history on the basis of the principle of *cause and effect.*

(2) An attempt should be made correlate the events of the post with the present social life.

(3) The books should be written in an interesting style.

(4) The language and style of the history book should be appropriate for the standard for which the books are meant.

(5) While writing the book, the writer should refrain from giving his personal opinion.

(6) The books should be well illustrated.

(7) The events that are described in the history books should be selected ones. The author should apply the 'principle of Selectivity' in prescribing the event. Only those events that have some bearing on the social life or are of interest for the students should be included in the

text-books.

Characteristics of the History Books According to Johnson

According to Johnson, the history books should be tested on the basis of pictures, maps and visual aids. While testing the quality of text-books, the teacher should keep the following things in mind:

(a) They should be clearly printed.

(b) They should be scaled to easy vision. It means that they should be interesting to the eyes of the students.

(c) They should be related to the text. It means that they should conform to the course prescribed for the particular class of students.

(d) The sources of the pictures and charts should be indicated. This will make the book authentic.

(8) The subject-material of the books should proceed from concrete to obstract and the subject-matter should be arranged on the basis of the 'principle of selectivity' of the organisation of the subject-material.

(9) The books should be nicely printed and their get-up, type and paper should be good and attractive.

(10) In the beginning of the book, there should be a list of content material.

(11) The whole subject-matter should be divided into various chapters. At the end of each chapter, there should be certain questions for recapitulation.

(12) The book should be reasonably priced and should be within the reach of common man.

(13) The style of the book should be in accordance with the age group of the students. For example, the books meant for the students of primary classes should be written in 'Story method'.

2. Maps

Maps are the universally accepted symbols which represent historical reality in space. They show the location, distance and direction of places connected with historical events. They give information about the distribution of land, water, vegetable life, climate, economic resources which have directly or indirectly shaped the destiny of man. They help to visualise historical realities and supplement their oral and written account.

Maps are of various kinds. Globe gives a three dimensional representation of the earth and may be conveniently used in showing historical events like World Wars I and II and other events of universal character. Relief maps are useful in showing the depressions and elevations on the surface of earth which have influenced the course of history. Invasions, military operations, migration of the people and social intercourse, all bear the impact of the inequalities in the surface of the earth. Flat maps showing physical features, political divisions, population, rainfall, temperature, soil, vegetation, means of transport and communication of the world and other countries provide ample opportunities for illustrating a history lesson.

The teacher tries to substantiate his statements and narration with the help of these maps. He tries to explain various places of historical importance with the help of these maps. Empires of various rulers may be indicated with the help of these maps.

The teacher has to use a pointer for indicating things on the maps. The pointer should be quite pointed at the end so that these may not be any confusion with regard to the location of the place, that the teacher wishes to point out.

The maps should be so drawn and coloured that they may be clearly visible to the students. Writing about maps a scholar says, "The map is not merely an aid to history teaching. It is as essential as in the fundamentals in other works are to be understood. Only through the use of maps can the area and relative positions of political units be visualized and make it possible to indicate the development of states. The progress of military campaigns or of exploration or the general distinction of religions and languages".

3. Pictures

To understand the physical and social activities of man in the background of his physical and natural environments pictures are quite useful. They give two dimensional representation to historical phenomenon and help in making history real. Besides presenting portraits of great personalities, pictures may be conveniently utilized to represent men and ideas. They can be used to represent the essential facts of history.

In recent years with tremendous developments in the field of science and technology, with the help of projectors, the teacher can create the third dimension illusion, sustain the interest of the pupils in the topic and enable them to understand the past happenings in their true setting.

Various types of pictures in use are:

(a) *Still pictures.* These are projected with the help of opaque projector, film strip projector, magic lantern etc.

(b) *Motion pictures.* They represent historical events in their proper perspective, showing their casual sequence and continuity. The emotional impact of such films is enormous and historical facts and events are remembered easily.

(c) *Films.* There are various types of films such as: (i) Class-room films, (ii) Documentary films etc. These films can bring into class-room such an element of realism which cannot be attained by any other medium of instruction.

(d) *Film strips or Film slides.* These are easy and simple to use. Many a film strips covering various parts of history are available. These are quite helpful to give the students useful knowledge of our history in an interesting way.

4. Charts

Various types of charts are drawn by the teacher on black-board while teaching history. Such charts may be classified as: (i) Table charts, (ii) Genealogical charts, (iii) Flow charts etc.

(i) Table Charts. They represent historical data in a tabular form and with their help the pupil gains a comprehensive view of the facts at a sight such charts facilitate comparison and contrast between different historical phenomenon.

(ii) Geneological Charts. Such charts are used to represent the growth and development of an empire, a dynasty or such other historical facts. They are quite useful in summarising historical topics.

(iii) Flow Charts. Such charts are generally used to represent organisational element and their functional relationship.

5. Magazines and Newspapers

Newspapers and magazines are the means of conveying the information about the current events. They also bring forth informations in regard to certain past events. They present various social and political problems before the people in greater detail.

Students of secondary classes must be encouraged to acquaint themselves with the political and social problems and movements with the help of the newspapers and magazines. They have the following advantages:

(i) Newspapers and magazines broaden the outlook of the students. they develop their power of understanding. They also give them an idea of the systematic representation of the subject-matter.

(ii) They enrich the knowledge of the students and they get fully acquainted with the social and political movements of their state and country.

6. Black-Board or Chalk Board

It is one of the oldest and an important teaching aid. Black-boards have been in use since a long time but these days chalk boards are extensively used in teaching of history in place of black-boards. Making use of these boards teacher can illustrate many things. In the primary stage they can be used for presenting the subject-matter with illustrations. In the middle and secondary classes, these can be used to present various diagrams, charts, maps etc. It is a convenient and vehicle of illustration etc. Edgar Dale says, "It provides an opportunity for creativity and initiative, as one 'Visualises' an explanation or a 'demonstration'. Its purpose is to visualise curriculum by means of graphic demonstration".

Illustrations. These are the material aids. They are of three types:

(i) Verbal illustration: These are the oral examples presented as stories etc.

(ii) Symbolic illustration: They are mall structures which are presented as symbols of certain historical facts and events.

(iii) Visual illustration: They refers to such things as charts, models, diagrams, pictures etc.

7. Models

Since original materials are scarce and rare and even those that exist are beyond the reach of all schools, the history teacher may take the help of models to give as vivid a picture of historical objects as possible. *Model* is nothing but a replica of a thing that we want to present or explain. It makes the teaching of history interesting and gives concrete idea of the abstract things. Models can be used to depict different aspects of human life—political, economic, social, religious and cultural.

Making of models provides an opportunity for 'learning by doing' and enlivens the interest of the pupils in the topic. Models prepared by the students or purchased from the market should be properly labelled, mounted and displayed. Labels should be short and self-explanatory.

Qualities of a Model

(i) It should be simple to understand.

(ii) It should be useful.

(iii) It should be accurately drawn.

8. Graphs

Graphs are used for representing quantitative data showing comparison, trends, developments and relationships. With the help of simple lines, drawn vertically or horizontally, graphs supply visual imageries for abstract ideas and concepts in history. In the teaching of history the following kinds of graphs may conveniently be used:

(a) Time Line. Time line gives linear representation of time. Time is the most abstract concept in history. Time line helps the pupils to gain time sense with the help of space symbols. An event happens at a particular time in history and at a particular place. We are interested to know its exact location on the long and unending line of time. In a time line, the length of time is symbolically represented by a line drawn horizontally of vertically. It gives a visual image of the sequence of events and their relative difference in their occurrence in time. It also helps us in comparing and contrasting and showing mutual relationship between events and happening at different places but at the same time.

(b) Hitsogram. Histogram represents an idea with the help of broad lines or narrow rectangles, drawn vertically or horizontally. The scale

of values is placed at the bottom in horizontal and at the left in a vertical arrangement. The broad lines of rectangles may be coloured or differentiated in some other ways. Histograms may be used to represent growth and fall of empires or some other historical phenomena.

(c) Pictorial Graph. Pictorial graph expresses an idea or a concept with the help of picture symbols which are self-explanatory and appropriate. The symbols generally used are man, ship, horse, elephants, money, etc., and their total qualities are shown by proper number or multiple of the symbols.

9. Diagrams

Diagrams represent historical facts and events with the help of visual symbols that convey a number of things within a short space and time. They help to present historical data in an interesting way and captivate attention of the pupils. Many themes such as, sources of history, important battles, administrative systems, comparison and contrast between religions, life in early civilisations may be diagramatically presented.

10. Posters

Posters are generally used for commercial purposes. They show pictures of peoples and objects. They can also give symbolic expression to ideas concerning local history. They can throw light on many aspects of human history.

11. Flash Cards

These are the cards on which written documents are printed in bold letters. Such cards are presented with the help of projector as a flash and students get a glance on them and comprehend the idea given in them. This technique introduces a dramatic element in teaching and captivates the attention of the pupils.

12. Bulletin Board

It is a display board and has great value for the teaching of history. It is used for displaying pictures, drawings, compositions, posters, photographs, news paper clippings. Such bulletin boards can be specified for specific branches or topics in history. Such a board should be fixed at a conspicuous place in the history room. The material displayed should be directly concerned with the activities of the pupils. An effort be made to change the material on bulletin board as frequently as practicable. Whenever teacher starts a new topic he may ask the students to display the concerned material on the bulletin board and the teacher should specifically mention to the students the display material on the board while teaching a topic to the class. Students be asked to take the charge of bulletin board by rotation.

13. Flannel Board

It is also sometimes referred to as flannel graph or felt board. It is made of wood, card board or straw board with colour led flannel or woollen cloth. It can be used as an effective teaching device in teaching of history. It can be used by the teacher to place various objects such as pictures, 'cut-outs' from news papers or magazines etc.

How to Use a Flannel Board

Following points be kept in mind for effective use of flannel board:

(i) The teacher should collect a large number of pictures or wall cut diagrams etc., and make use of these one by one after proper selection.

(ii) Display the material on the flannel board in a sequence to develop the lesson.

(iii) Make proper use of flannel board in a sequence to develop the lesson.

(iv) Change the material on the board as frequently as possible.

(v) Flannel board can be used quite effectively for showing relationship between different parts or steps of a process.

Advantages of Flannel Board

Some of the advantages of flannel board are as under;

(i) It is quite economical and easy to handle and operate.

(ii) The pictures or cuttings can be easily fixed and removed when required without spoiling the material. Thus the same material can be used for display many a times.

(iii) Any display material on the board hold the interest of students and arrests their attention.

(iv) Such boards enable a teacher to talk alongwith changing illustrations to develop a lesson.

14. Radio

Radio can serve as an effective aid in teaching of history. The broad-casts from experts can be easily made available to all children. They transcend the limitations of space. All India Radio has in its regular features some programmes meant for school children. In such programmes generally talks on educational matters are broadcasted. The topic, date and time of such broadcast are given in advance by A.I.R. They touch many aspects in history of India. They throw light on the life of personalities who have shaped the history of our country. There are also light programmes consisting of music, drama, comics etc. There are also general broadcasts about important speeches and declarations of important personalities on important occasions.

To make a best use of all these talks and broadcasts the following points be kept in mind:

(i) The school broadcasts should be integrated with class-work and class projects.

(ii) Every school broadcast should serve as the starting point of discussion between the teacher and the pupil.

(iii) To derive the maximum benefit, from such a talk, the class should be supplied with ample supporting literature generously illustrated.

Advantages

(i) The radio broadcasts are of high intellectual and educational value and help in ordering the mental horizon of the children.

(ii) It brings dramatic feeling into the class-room.

(iii) It transcends the limitation of time and space.

(iv) It provides an opportunity to the students for coming in contact with great personalities through their voices.

(v) It gives the pupils a sense of participation.

(vi) It facilitates group instructions.

Limitations

(i) When the receiving set is not working satisfactorily a sense of strain prevails in the class-rome.

(ii) Some students are poor listeners and may not be benefited by such talks.

Keeping in view the utility of radio broadcasts UNESCO has recommended that compulsory arrangement for a radio set should be made in every school and radio broadcasts be directed for this purpose.

15. Television

The role of television in the present day world is becoming more and more important as a teaching aid. In it the advantages of radio and film are combined. These days U.G.C. programmes are a regular feature on 'Door Darshan'.

It is "medium of mass communication which far surpasses in effectiveness anything our civilisation has yet known." It accomplishes certain communicative tasks which are incomparable in their effectiveness.

Television, with its two-fold engagement of the eye and the ear, like the motion pictures, can bring us into contact with events in an exciting and clarifying way. It is a "means by which teachers, parents, children, and all citizens may share a common experience at the same time." It is a versatile vehicle to use a beauty of audio-visual materials.

The potentialities of television in history teaching are enormous. It can transport the places and sites of historical importance which the pupils are unable to visit. It can bring the experts in the classroom not only in voice but in person. It can make available to the classroom rare examples of natural or man-made objects.

16. Films and Cinema

Today cinema is a very powerful agency of propagation of ideas and knowledge. Through it, knowledge can be disseminated very effectively. It also brings about recreation and so the students do not feel bored while acquiring knowledge through cinema or films.

In foreign countries, films on historical events and historical places are made and they are exhibited in the classrooms as well as in the picture halls. They are generally called documentaries.

Coins and other historical material can also form the subject-matter of the films.

17. Cinema Projectors

This is the mechanism through which the films are exhibited. If the History laboratory has a light weight cinema projector, small films may be exhibited in the class and this shall be of great use to the students.

Johnsons has laid good deal of stress on the use of films in the teaching of history. He said: Dozens of historical film have stirred children to ask historical questions and when such questions are brought to school, almost' any teacher is likely to suggest it best to the children 'look it up in some history or encylopaedia'."

Eddison has gone a step further. He thinks, the films in themselves can serve the purpose of the teachers. He has remarked, "Films are inevitable as practically the sole Teaching method".

18. Epidiascope

It is a costly instrument and is used to project opaque objects as well as transparent objects. The pictures projected are much brighter and needs a less powerful light and the need of absolutely dark room is not there.

The name *epidiascope* is given to it because it works as an *episode* when it is used to throw an image of an opaque object. When it is used to project a slide it works as a *diascope* and so *epidiascope* is a combination of the two.

Advantages of Epidiascope

(i) It can be operated in a room which may not be absolutely dark.

(ii) It can project the original colours of the pictures or photographs.

(iii) The projection or the screen can be kept for sometime during which teacher can explain it and discuss it in the class.

(iv) It provides the teacher an option to handle the lesson according to himself.

19. Museum

A museum ought to be a very valuable part of history department in school. Museum not only provides necessary help in teaching but also helps in creating the right type of atmosphere in the school. The importance of museum has nicely been summarised by a scholar, "It is true that the wealth of painting, music, sculpture, dress, industries, tools and religious outlook, all the significant phases of life that are well-illustrated in the important museums of the land, cannot be adequately represented in the school history museum, but an attempt must be made to put in a variety of materials to be used as aids which will help the imagination to picture the life that is gone, and yet at the same time, influences the present in a subtle though in a very real way."

In the organization of museum both teacher and students have to take an active part. They should help the following points in mind:

(i) Systematic arrangement of various exhibits.

(ii) Clear and complete description of various parts of an exhibit.

For this purpose an ideal arrangement will be that a card of suitable size (5" × 4") be attached, to each exhibit, containing the following information typed on it:

(i) Name of the exhibit.

(ii) Place from where the exhibit has been obtained and relevant information.

(iii) Importance of the exhibit.

The language used to provide above information should be simple and all efforts be made to avoid phrases and technical terms in the description of the exhibit.

20. Tours and Excursions

Excursions and trips provide an opportunity for the direct study of original materials in history. Visits to places of worship, tombs etc., help to break the monotony of class-room lectures and provide a chance to come in direct contact with historical realities.

It has been said that "History is the action and reaction of nature and thought." In other words, it means that history should be studied in the light of the effect of various events that have their reaction on the social life.

For organising such trips the teacher should survey various local possibilities and then should carefully plan all the details of the trip or excursion and then during such a trip he should see that every detail of the plan is adhered to. The trip should be held in an informal atmosphere. During the trip or immediately afterwards the teacher should try to correlate the experiences gained to the history lessons.

An evaluation of the trip is essential. For this teacher should invite comments and remarks. Such as evaluation will provide basis for other trips and help in the removal of their shortcomings.

Advantages

(i) It makes class-room teaching interesting.

(ii) It helps to develop love for cultural heritage.

(iii) It helps to develop a sense of patriotism.

(iv) It helps in the development of the knowledge of local history.

(v) It helps to develop mental faculties and powers.

REVISION QUESTIONS

(1) Prepare a list of the teaching aids, which you consider absolutely essential for the successful teaching of History. Give reasons as well.

(2) Mention in detail the devices you would employ in the teaching of History in order to make the past 'real.'

(3) Describe the various devices you would use for making the past real in the teaching of history.

Chapter 10

Teaching of Time Sense in History

10.1 INTRODUCTION

A history teacher finds the task of cultivation of time and space sense and imagination development amongst his pupils as the most complicated and a difficult problem. Time and space being two most abstract concepts in history. All the events of history have occurred at a definite place and a definite time so history devoid of the sense of time and place is nothing but a story, similarly, development of historical imagination is also an equally important task. A history teacher should therefore try to develop among the pupils the capacity to see every historical event in its time perspective.

10.2 MEASURING OF TIME SENSE

Time sense refers to the capacity through which we are able to establish a lively relationship between the various events. In fact, time is focal point or some definite point. It helps in understanding the flow of various events of society in the order they come to pass.

Elements of Time Sense

Location, distance and duration are the three elements which constitute time relations.

(a) The Location of Time. Most of the historical facts are localised and not indefinite. Location of an event refers to its placing on the long line of time so that it may enable as to measure its distance from us. By location we mean determining the events with the help of dates and periods. For having a time sense we have following agencies:

(a) Time chart, (b) Time line, and (c) Time graph.

(b) Time Chart. It consists of a list of pictures pasted on it (paper or chart) indicating the description of a particular dynasty. Following lines clarify this point:

> "The main use of time chart is to provide a chronological framework within which events and developments may be recorded and to guard against the vagueness of time sense which may result from teaching arranged, often necessarily by 'topics' rather than by 'reigns'."

Panorama charts depicts one event of one century e.g. To depicts 19th century we may depicts First War for independence, of 1857.

Time charts be drown on certain scale, they should be attractive and drawn in a scientific manner.

(c) Time Line. It is quite helpful in developing time sense in an effective and easy way. It provides the pupils a scientific knowledge about the dates of history.

Time line be prepared to represent a few dates carefully selected. Time lines may be either *progressive time line* or *Regressive time line*.

To draw a time line following procedure is generally followed:

Draw a line 20 centimeters long to represent a century and divide it into ten equal parts which will indicate units of ten years.

The figure for each unit of 10 years will be written on the left side of the line. On the right side, the dates which are considered most important will be marked at suitable points.

(d) Time Graph. It is also used for development of time sense. It can be used for making a comparative study of certain events. It can also be used to show the comparative down fall of two dynasties.

In drawing a time graph, we may take a line of 3 to 4 centimetres in length. Each centimetre may indicate 10 years and so this line shall indicate 3 to 4 centuries. We can sort out certain dates on this line. On special dates and places, certain straight or perpendicular lines may be drawn. They should be indicative of the development of the English Rule in the Indian sub-continent.

Requisites of time line and time graph. Following are the requisites of time line and time graph:

(1) Time line and time graphs should be drawn with great caution. An attempt should be made to see that the dates are accurate. While

drawing graphs, it should be borne in mind that the line does not go very high.

(2) Time line and time graph should be artistically drawn. III-drawn figures shall scare away the students from history. If these graphs are nicely drawn, the students shall be attracted towards them and they shall try to look at them carefully.

(3) The students should be associated with drawing of these figures.

(4) These things should be explained elaborately to the students. Their explanation is difficult than their drawing. Aims of these things is to develop time sense in the students and therefore, their explanation should be properly done.

Since this is a difficult task, only those teachers who are interested in the teaching of history can do these things properly.

Walls of the history class or the 'history laboratory' should be decorated with these time charts and time graphs. They shall provide decorative as well as study material for the students.

The teachers should put questions to the students in regard to these devices.

Forms of the Time Line Charts. Time line charts may be of the following forms:

(1) Prependicular form, (2) Circular form, (3) Straight line form, and (4) Peak form.

10.3 MEANING OF SPACE SENSE

Space sense refers to the capacity of the individual to comprehend the place relations of historical phenomenon. It is an understanding of the places located on the surface of the earth or on other planets where man on his long march down the ages, has settled, cultivated the soil, fought battles, etc. The *location, direction* and *distance* from the basic elements of our space sense.

The cultivation of space sense is comparatively easier than the time sense. The place relation of historical facts offer more tangible things to work with their time relationship. Johnson say, "the experience of seeing or walking a mile down the road has a line of physical reality denied to the thirty minutes which it may take a child to walk a mile down". The teaching of place relations will, however, require ingenuity and strenuous effort on the part of the teacher. For this purpose he can make use of various devices such as maps, place charts, layer charts etc.

Maps

Map is the most commonly used symbol for the representation of space. It shows location, direction, distance; extent, area, land and water forms. It conveys information about distribution of people, animal and vegetable life, climate, economic resources, etc. It also indicates the extent of territories, areas of political control, routes of movement of armies, travels, and so on. It also helps us in visualising important historical happenings which would not have been possible for us to understand the appreciate properly from their oral and written accounts. Thus maps are the sure means of concretising historical happenings and help in the understanding of the historical phenomena with reference to their place of occurrence.

From their very birth children being to experience persons and objects around them. They note their size, location, differences and relationships and meanings in order to deal with them successfully. Maps give expression to these through visual symbols. From the very beginning of their school instruction pupils should be initiated in the art of drawing maps. First of all the teacher should try to make the pupil familiar with general lay out of the map drawing. He should give them the idea of directions, scale and other symbols. After this preliminary knowledge pupils should be asked to draw map of their own locality and in this way as the area of their experience widens they will take to the drawing of the sketch maps of their town, their province, their country and finally of the world. But at every stage the need is that they got a clear understanding of location' distance and direction.

Place Charts

The concept of distance and direction can be greatly clarified by drawing lines from their home town or from a particular place of historical occurrence. We may call this resulting diagram a place chart. It may be constructed within a blackboard or on the outline map of a country or of the world or as lines without any map. Exercises of this kind help the pupils to have an idea of the distances and directions of the places mentioned in the history lesson. They also help the pupils to have an idea of "Where he is in history while he is there".[1]

Layer Charts

It is an interesting device for showing the growth of a kingdom or an empire. For this a thick paper of the same size of the map is taken and the portion under each rule is cut. These papers may be pinned or stitched in one side, one over the other and thereby will show the territories under each ruler over the other. By lifting each sheet and then allowing it to fall, the pupils would get a good idea of the addition made by a ruler or the loss suffered by him in regard to territories.

Cultivation of Historical Imagination

History is the study of past human actions and more particularly with the motives, intentions, purposes, designs and policies which prompted human beings to behave in a particular way. The human actions of the past societies are not available for direct observation. They can simply be inferred or apprehended through the imaginative powers of mind.

Historical imagination refers to the capacity of an individual to visualise scenes and incidents as narrated to him through spoken or written word. It is also the capacity of an individual to draw inferences about past events to form mental pictures of the past happenings and to try to find the meaning hidden behind past human actions. The essence of history teaching lies in the encouragement of the powers of historical imagination of the pupils who are anxious to know about other people, about their lives, personalities, deeds and ideas. It can help them to visualise an atmosphere, entirely different from their own. It can awaken in them an imaginative wonder and excitement about the lives and actions of the people down the ages. And finally, it will help them to create an abiding interest and reverence in all things which are the relics of the past ages.

The cultivation of historical imagination is a difficult task. He should also see that his descriptions of places, persons and things are

1. Henry, Johnson, *Teaching of History*, p. 101.

graphic and are communicated through vivid word-pictures. In fact at this stage of life children usually possess a riotous imagination. The need is to channelize this imagination in desired direction.

In the upper grades our aim should be to help the pupil not only to see what happened in the past, but enable him to understand why it happened. Not only should he be introduced to the understanding of the causal relationships between different historical phenomena but he should be asked to visualise the intentions, purposes and designs behind those phenomena. This kind of understanding depends on inside view of human nature. The teacher should try to develop this understanding. "The human mind can understand whatever it has created and the whole historical world spreads before us as a field of human activity, of the realisation of human hopes and the suffering, of misery and frustration by human beings." He should be allowed to think and re-think in his mind and use his imagination to recapture the spirit of the age.

REVISION QUESTIONS

1. What do you understand by Time Sense in history ? What will you do to cultivate time sense in the pupils ?
2. What are the basic constituents of Time Sense ? Explain them with examples.
3. What is the meaning of Space Sense ? How can it be developed in the students ?
4. What is the Historical Imagination ? How will you cultivate historical imagination among your pupils ?
5. What steps will you follow in teaching chronology to the pupils ? Discuss with examples.

Chapter 11

History Teacher

11.1 INTRODUCTION

The success or failure of a course in history rests mainly with the teacher. The most important factor in entire educational programme is the teacher. It is the teacher on whom the real success or failure of any method, aid, device or procedure depends. It is he who can evaluate how far the aims, and objectives of teaching have been achieved. The history teacher not only deals with the successes and failures of the man in the past but also of the current and recurrent events and happenings of the world of today and so he is of special importance. Lord R. Bryce has rightly observed, "The teacher of history must have the power of realising the date passed in a living present and have a touch of imagination as well as vastly large amount of positive knowledge, then he will attempt to pile upon the memory of his class".

In this regard the Kothari Commission report (1966) says, "of all the different factors which influence the quality of education and its contribution to national development, the quality, competence and character of teachers are undoubtedly the most significant".

The role of teacher has been emphasized by Dr. S. Radhakrishnan in the following words, "The teacher's place in society is of vital importance. He acts as the pivot for transmission of intellectual traditions and technical skill from generation to generation, and helps to keep the lamp of civilisation burning. He not only guides the individual, but also, so to say, the destiny of nation. Teachers have, therefore, to realise their special responsibility to the society. On the other hand, it is incumbent on the society to pay due regard to the teaching profession and to ensure that the teacher is kept above want and given the status which will command respect from his students".

In order to achieve all the objects, the teacher of history must have some qualities and specific qualifications.

11.2 QUALITIES AND QUALIFICATIONS OF A HISTORY TEACHER

A history teacher is expected to possess certain academic qualifications as also certain professional qualifications.

As regards the academic qualifications it is usually a pass in matriculation/senior secondary examination for becoming a history teacher in a primary school. A pass in B.A. examination for being a teacher in history in a middle or high school and a pass in M.A. examination for being a teacher in a senior secondary school (grades 11 and 12).

In addition to the above academic qualifications, any one who wish to be appointed as a history teacher has to undergo a teachers training course (i.e., either G.B.T. or B.T./B.Ed.). This professional training is all the more important these days when new techniques of teaching, evaluation etc., are being introduced. Trained teachers also require the stimulus of a refresher course to keep themselves informed about the latest methods of teaching and to refresh his knowledge of history. All this is quite essential because a good teacher must always keep him self-informed of the latest development in the field. This aspect of teacher has been brought out in the following words by Dr. Rabinder Nath Tagore, "A teacher can never truly teach unless he is still learning himself. A lamp cannot light another lamp unless it continues to burn its own flame".

11.3 CHARACTERISTICS OF AN IDEAL HISTORY TEACHER

A successful history teacher must have the following qualities:

1. Thorough Knowledge of the Subject

Like the teacher of any other subject a history teacher should have a thorough knowledge of the subject. For such a knowledge the teacher should read various reference books in addition to the prescribed text-books. Such a study will help the teacher to grasp the spirit of the subject and study it in a proper perspective. The continuity in study is also essential to keep the knowledge of the subject upto date. It is not essential that a secondary school teacher be a specialist of his subject but it is essential that he should be able to present the facts of history in a psychological manner. For such a presentation teacher should be aware of the fact that social sciences are a developing subject.

2. Knowledge of Child Psychology

For being a successful teacher in any subject a knowledge of child psychology is essential and so is the case with history teacher. The psychological requirements of child differ from age to age and a teacher must have a thorough knowledge of child psychology if he wish to impart the knowledge of the subject in a proper manner. Thus the knowledge of child psychology and its proper use can contribute a lot in teaching of history.

3. Faith in Subject

Unless a teacher has faith in his subject, he will not be able to acquire thorough knowledge of it. This faith also encourages the teacher to learn more and more. This faith also enables the teacher to realise the utility and the value of teaching history.

4. Knowledge of Different Methods of Teaching

The knowledge of various methods of teaching is essential because it is only then possible to choose a suitable method according to the requirements of a particular class, e.g., a student at the age of 14 is fond of excursions and travels and a good teacher knowing it can co-ordinate the two in his teaching method to make the teaching successful.

5. Knowledge of Regional and Provincial History

In addition to thorough knowledge of history of our country, a good history teacher must have a good knowledge of regional and provincial history. While teaching history he should give examples from this history.

6. Knowledge of Current Events

Such a knowledge helps the teacher in making a comparative study of the events of various periods, in the history of different countries of the world.

7. Knowledge of Aims and Objectives of Teaching of History

The history teacher should have clear knowledge of the aims and objectives of the teaching of history. The teacher must also have a faith in these aims and objectives. With such a faith, he becomes interested in the subject and tries to impart knowledge in a scientific and interesting manner to suit the students and society both.

8. Originality

A history teacher should never feel satisfied by reading what others say but should be in a position to form his own independent judgement of men and affairs. He must not have a blind faith, rather he should make it a habit to inquire to find the truth. If he possesses such qualities he can face any class-room situation that may arise unexceptionally under various circumstances.

9. Sympathetic, Creative Imagination and Ability to Act

The history teacher should have a sympathetic out-look. It is essential for presenting the historical facts in an impartial and scientific manner without sympathy, it is impossible for the teacher to understand the perspective of the developments of history.

He should also be endowed with 'Creative Imagination'. Creative imagination enables the teacher of history to present the facts and the events in a lively manner to his students. This helps him to have the proper understanding of the facts and enables him to present them in a lively and interesting manner.

Unless the teacher of history has some touch of an acting in him, he cannot bring to life the past, in the classroom. The teacher has to modulate his voice and present things in such a way that the events may look like real.

10. Broad Outlook and Strong Memory

The teacher of history must have a broad out-look and strong memory, so that he is able to have proper knowledge and assessment of the events and facts of the past. Sharp memory enables him to remember the details. All these things will make the teaching of history interesting and successful. Prof. K.D. Ghosh observed, "Teacher of history is likely to be guided by his personal likes and dislikes".

"History teacher colours teaching of history, his interpretation of incidents and personality with his own likes or dislikes born of the religious denominations to which he belongs."

Actually, the teacher of history should try to rise above the situation. If he colours his teaching with his likes and dislikes and with the views of his religion, the teaching of history will lose its value in a Secular state. The trend of society and the requirements of the members should also be kept in mind.

11. Impressive and Interesting Personality

The teacher of history should have an impressive and interesting personality. If he lacks these then he shall not be able to present the facts in an effective manner. The teacher of history quite often has to play the role of an actor. A person without an impressive and interesting personality shall make himself only a laughing stock if he takes to acting. This element of personality should also be accompanied by certain other traits. According to Prof. K.D. Ghosh:

"While an interesting personality is one of the important facts in a successful effective lesson, it is very doubtful if the teacher with personality would have a continuous success in his lesson unless he has a proper grip over the method, i.e., methods of teaching."

According to Bryce:

"He has to do as much talking as is necessary for fulfilling his fundamental duty of making things vivid, clear, and kindling a love for the subject."

12. Responsible Social Worker

Since the history teacher has to serve coming generations with his social service so his role is more or less of a responsible social worker. He can be said to have achieved his task if he has been able to would the lives of young ones in the right direction.

13. A Good Story Teller

Story-telling is an art and it is most desirable thing to be possessed by a history teacher. A good history teacher should be capable of framing stories connected with different historical aspects and present such stories to his students in an interesting way. This quality is more desirable in a history teacher teaching lower classes. It makes him a very successful teacher.

14. Capacity to Undertake Excursions and Tours

The teaching of history requires that the students should be taken out on tours and execursions to the places of historical importance. It is the teacher of history who has to accompany the students in order to explain the things to them. The teacher of history should be capable of undertaking and understanding things.

15. Capacity to Arrange and Decorate the History Room

In the modern education the need of a separate history room or history class has been well-emphasised. A history room cannot be established and furnished unless the teacher of history is anxious to furnish and decorate it. In fact, in the teaching of history, a good deal of importance is given to a history room. The history room should be equipped with black-board, historical pictures, charts and other materials.

A teacher of history, in the words of Prof. E.L. Husluck should have the following qualities:

> "History requires a teacher who is willing to be ever active, ever inquiring, ever on his guard against the numerous fit falls which beset his path. He may take as his motto that of our 'ducal houses covendo huts."

11.4 PROBLEMS FACED BY HISTORY TEACHER

A number of problems baffle an ordinary history teacher. Some of these are as under:

1. Scanty Knowledge of History

An ordinary history teacher is generally not much interested in his subject and he is not quite enthusiastic to supplement his knowledge of history that he acquired in the school/college age. He is neither interested in reading nor in excursions. He is not interested to train himself in a scientific way. He generally has wrong notions about historical facts and it leads to a disastrous situation. Such a teacher is likely to present distorted facts to the pupils and thus distort their personality.

2. Lacks the Knowledge of World History

Generally history teachers in our schools are found lacking in the knowledge of world history. Due to this lack of knowledge they fail to view the historical facts in their real prospective. Every social or political movement in any part of the world has its effect on the entire world, so it is not possible for anyone to deal with the history of his country quite exclusively. Thus the knowledge of world history is a must for any successful history teacher, without it his teaching will remain imperfect.

3. Religious or Social Bias

Most of the teacher suffer from such a bias and any one suffering from it cannot provide the currect knowledge of history. If a Hindu teacher is fanatic and has racial bias he cannot teach the history of Muslims period correctly and impartially. He shall definitely be dishonest in teaching because it would be quite difficult for him to explain how the Muslims pondered over the Hindu rulers. Similar situation will exist for teacher of other religions.

4. National Bias

In the teaching of history, national bias is as harmful as the religious or racial bias. "My country, right or wrong" is a condemned slogan. Patriotism has great virtues and one should be patriotic but patriotism and national bias have different meanings. A true patriot sees and confesses the weaknesses of his country while a person who has national bias cannot do this. A teacher of history suffering from national bias shall never explain before the children the weaknesses of his country. If a history teacher in India has national bias, he shall not explain before the children that the Britishers were able to have their rule in this country due to the weaknesses of his own countrymen. On the other hand, he will tell the students that there were no weaknesses in Indian rulers and it was the mere cunningness of Britishers that they dominated over the Indians. A history teacher should be patriotic but he should never have national bias. He should try to develop the international understanding in himself and his people.

5. Faulty Method of Teaching

In our country history is generally considered to deal with dead princes and bygone events and such a teaching will become lifeless. However, history is a living subject as it deals with 'drama of the human beings or the stage of the world which is still growing on'. This drama should be presented before the children in a vivid manner in class-room. For this a history teacher should be active and full of life.

6. Lack of Correlation

Most of the teachers teaching history fail to correlate history with other subjects. Since no subject can be taught in isolation so history should never be taught in such a manner. It is always possible for the history teacher to correlate his subject with geography, civics, economics or craft or any other subject.

11.5 HOW TO MAKE HISTORY TEACHING REALISTIC

To inculcate the interest of students in history and to make history teaching realistic, the following points he kept in mind:

1. Correlation with the Other Subjects

In order to make the teaching of history interesting and realistic, it is of great importance to correlate the subject with other subjects. We have discussed this Correlation in Chapter XII of this book Correlation of history with subjects make it interesting and meaningful. Historical novels, if exploited skillful, help us to a great extent in providing the knowledge of history, to the people. They create an atmosphere and environment of the previous ages easily. In the same way, correlation with geography proves useful and helps in understanding the background of most of the historical facts.

2. Excursions to the Sites of Historical Interest

As we have already said that today the world is not as it was about 200 or 400 years ago. However, there are places of historical interests where we can get the same atmosphere as it was during old age. So, the execursions to the sites of historical importance are very useful in the teaching of history, and it will make our lessons interesting and realistic. Old historical sites, ruins and buildings are the real and original sources of history. They help us a lot in understanding the past and so such excursions are most important for the teaching of history.

3. Dramatization

Dramatization is another valuable device which makes the lessons of history interesting and effective. This device fixes the historical events in memory and helps in creating the real atmosphere of bygone ages. The students who had acted as Maharana Pratap understand the great hero more than an ordinary teacher of history. A student who has seen Chandra Gupta, can learn more about Chandra Gupta than the student who has not seen him in actión.

4. Use of Audio-visual Aids

Use of audio-visual aids can also make the teaching of history interesting and realistic. These aids are meant for making the history teaching lively and useful. Films and cinema, radio, cinema projectors and television can make our subject more realistic, and so a teacher should utilise these aids upto the maximum extent.

5. Maps

Use of maps also make the teaching of history effective. The teacher tries to substantiate his statement with the help of these maps. If he can explain the various places of historical importance and the empires of the various rulers with the help of maps, the lesson becomes more interesting. In fact, map is not merely an aid to history teaching but it is essential and we cannot ignore it.

6. Collateral Reading

Collateral reading should also be encouraged while teaching history. It develops the understanding of the subject. It fills in the gaps in the knowledge.

All the points mentioned above will be of no use if the history teacher lacks the qualities desired in a good history teacher. Actually speaking it is the competent teacher who creates an atmosphere for his pupils to roam in past and thus make the teaching of history interesting.

11.6 TEACHER'S RELATIONSHIP WITH HIS PUPILS, COLLEAGUES AND THE COMMUNITY

In relation to his pupils, a teachers must be of friendly co-operation and sympathetic understanding. If he takes genuine interest in his pupils, he will certainly command faith, loyalty and respect. He must mix with them, play with them, participate in various activities and encourage them on all occasions. He must pay individual attention towards the backward, abnormal and problem students.

With other members of the staff also, he must cultivate intimate relationship. He must always be obliging and co-operating because all are engaged in a common task. He must give his colleagues helping hand whenever required because teaching is a co-operative enterprise. He must neither back-bite nor interfere unnecessarily in their affairs. He should especially work closely with the administration and be obedient and loyal. He should, no doubt, enjoy academic freedom, but he should be careful not to do anything that will reflect upon his position as a teacher.

In relation of community, a teacher should feel himself responsible to the whole society. He should remember that school is an agency that society has set up to instruct its young members. He, therefore, has an obligation to the parents of his pupils and to the community at large. He should remember that both home and school are engaged in a co-operative task. He must, therefore, welcome contacts and conference with parents on various occasions in the interest of the education of the pupils. The more he understands and serves the community, the better the teacher.

REVISION QUESTIONS

1. What should be the essential qualities of a history teacher ?
2. Why does history require the highest type of teacher ?
3. Why is general and liberal education necessary for a teacher of history ?
4. Write a short essay on "An Ideal History Teacher".
5. What do you consider to be the essential equipment of a successful history teacher ?
6. Discuss the history teacher's relationship with his pupils and with his colleagues.

Chapter 12

History Room

12.1 INTRODUCTION

Like any other subject rooms there should be a separate room for history. The setting and arrangement of this room should be such that it creates an atmosphere for the study and teaching of history. The students entering the room would find themselves interested in the learning of history.

At present we have various types of teaching aids such as text-books, reference books, pamphlets, maps, charts, projectors, models, magazines etc., and there can be properly used if they are stored in a systematic way in a separate room called the history room. In fact a well equipped history room is essential for fostering a historical attitude of mind among the pupils.

12.2 ESSENTIAL EQUIPMENTS FOR A HISTORY ROOM

It would be desirable to have the history room a little bigger than an ordinary class-room. It should then be furnished and provided for carrying out various activities such as instructional work, demonstration, group works etc. For carrying out such activities the following material is essential for every history room.

I. Chalk Board

The colour of such a board may be green, yellow, white or even black. This is used to draw outline pictures as also to write summaries etc. It should be located at such a place that it can easily be seen by the students.

II. Bulletin Board

It is used to display maps, charts, current events, news-items, paper cuttings, magazine articles etc.

III. Furniture

Sufficient furniture for seating of the students be provided. It should also be provided with a movable desk or table and a chair for the teacher. In addition to this it should be provided with a table dictionary, desk calender, pen etc., for teachers use.

IV. Books and Book Cases

Text-books by different authors, current magazines, periodicals, reference books be provided in sufficient numbers so that students have an easy access to the reading material. Open-book shelves may be provided for storing these items.

V. Audiovisual Teaching Aids

The history room should be fully equipped with various types of audiovisual teaching aids such as pictures, maps, models, specimens, films, film-strips, globe etc. If possible provision should also be made to have projectors, record player, radio-set and tape recorder in the history room. There teaching aids play an important role in teaching of history.

VI. Collections

A corner in the history room be reserved for old coins, old clothes, dresses, utencils, historical relics, old paintings, art pictures etc. Such items may be got collected through history students.

Flags of different nations be also exhibited in the history room. It need be a brief history of such flags may also be tagged with the flags.

VII. History Room

History room should also be provided with paints, water colours, coloured pencils, inks, pen-holders, brushes, rulers, compasses, erasers, scissors, blotters, special papers of different size and colour, paste, paper clips, drawing sets, pins, nails etc. All these things are needed by students for their practical work in history.

Advantages of History Room

Various advantages of a separate history room for the teaching of history are as under:

(1) Scientific Teaching. It helps to make it possible to bring about the scientific teaching of the subject.

(2) It Makes Teaching of History Effective. In the absence of a separate history room, the teacher has to carry the teaching aids and other materials with him. Such steps are not needed when there is a separate history room. It saves the spoiling of the material for the teaching of history, in the transit and also the time.

(3) Proper Atmosphere. It creates an atmosphere suitable and congenial for the teaching of history.

(4) It Develops the Power of Imagination and Observation. In a particularly equipped history room, there are maps, charts and other useful things for the teaching of history. These things help to develop power of observation and imagination of the students.

All these things are possible if the history room is properly equipped.

VIII. Cabinets and Files

Cabinets and files are required to store different materials. The filing system is helpful in locating the needed article at once.

The above points can be summarised as under:

(a) It should be spacious enough as to accommodate the students and have space for demonstrations, models, blackboard and charts etc.

(b) It should also have arrangement for acting certain dramas.

(c) There should be a good arrangement of blackboards. Teaching of history requires a lot of use of blackboards. There may be overlapping boards. Such arrangement would facilitate the drawing of charts and the maps.

(d) There should be a small collection of books in the history room.

(e) The history room should be decorated with the pictures of historical personalities and charts etc. There should also be pictures of the battles and wars and similar events.

(*f*) There should be arrangement of Epidiascope. There should also be arrangement of globes and project pictures.

It shall be useful to have a small historical museum. This museum should consist of the coins, clothes, dresses, utensils etc., of olden days. Models of these things would also serve a good purpose. There should also be devices for developing time sense in the students.

All these things can be arranged only if the teacher of history is competent and painstaking. Without hard labour on the part of the teacher, the teaching of history cannot be made lively and interesting.

12.3 CLASS-ROOM MANAGEMENT

The history room should be the place where a healthy social relationship develops between pupils and pupils and also between teacher and pupils. To achieve it students be given their due share in the management of the history room. Various committees be formed for purchase, collection, arrangement etc., and students be given a training for group leadership and committee co-operation through such committees.

In the words of Moffatt and Howell "Class-room management expresses a businesslike and orderly approach to the teaching-learning situation. Leadership gives direction and provides for the type of atmosphere so essential for effective instruction. Good organisation for all activities eliminates confusion and possible discipline problems. Pupils should, therefore, be encouraged to develop abilities and attitude commensurate with the democratic sharing of responsibilities in the co-management of their own class-room." Good work should be appreciated and each student should be encouraged to show his worth. Opportunities for self-discipline and self-control, based on co-operation, should be provided to all pupils. This will lead to character building and personal development. If our students assume responsibilities in the true spirit and discharge them to the best of their abilities and capacities, they are receiving effective training for democratic citizenship.

12.4 LABORATORY-WORK IN HISTORY

Besides regular history periods provided in the school time-table, some periods be allotted for *laboratory work* in history. The basic purpose of laboratory work is to develop skills, original thinking, planning and to develop creative expression among students. In the laboratory-work period students are busy in drawing maps, preparing graphs, charts, time lines, models or pictures, solving problems, working on projects and answering given questions and assignments individually or in groups. Specific instructions are given to students regarding the work to be done and sources from where the material is to be collected. They try to learn through research and exploration. They are given freedom to move about the class-room and make maximum possible use of the material, pertaining to the work in hand. Although time is fixed for the completion of each activity or unit, yet the students are allowed to progress according to their own ability and capacity.

In these work periods the teacher acts as a guide and a director. He gives suggestion, guidance, encouragement and help when the pupils are in difficulty. It is his duty to see that the pupils achieve their goal with the least wastage of time and energy. Laboratory work provides the kind of social relationship in which both the pupils and the teacher plan, work, study and learn together. They may be working individually or in groups, but the feeling is that all engaged in a task leading to a common goal.

12.5 HISTORY MUSEUM

In every school or college, there should be a museum in which the material of historical importance should be kept. In the lower classes, there is no need for a separate history museum. However, there should be a museum in which old coins, pieces of architecture etc., should be placed along with the other materials. For the higher secondary and degree colleges, there should be a separate room for the history museum in which all the available material of historical importance should be placed.

The museum helps a lot in the teaching of history. The students when visit the museum, are easily acquainted with the historical species which develop their knowledge of history. The students should be encouraged to collect the material for the history museum. However, the teacher should take care that only those things are kept in museum which are really of the historical importance. If the teacher is not conscious in this respect, the whole purpose of the museum will be spoiled and it would not serve the purpose of educating the young ones in the right perspective.

REVISION QUESTIONS

1. What is the need for a history room?
2. List the main equipment of a history room.
3. Give in brief the management of a history room.
4. Explain the importance of laboratory work in history.

Chapter 13

History Library

13.1 INTRODUCTION

History is quite a vast subject. A history teacher should not follow only the text-book and be must study some standard books from the library. It will provided him a deeper insight into the subject and thorough command of the same. The teacher will be able to plan and organise his teaching in a better way, better than that given in the text-books.

History library is quite useful to the students. When students read or consult some books from the library, their doubts become clear. Moreover, the study of library books acquaints them with new exercises or problems and prepares them better for the examination. A good history library also helps inculcating proper attitudes, interests and appreciations in the students. It can acquaint them with historical background of different topic and the contributions of various personalities.

Library Facilities in Schools

In our schools there are two types of libraries :

(a) General school library; and

(b) History department library.

(a) General School Library

In most of our schools there is a general school library which contains books and magazines an all subjects. Then there should be separate sections for history books. For the teachers there should be good books on methodology of teaching, contributions of various historians and important historical personalities. For students there should be books on recreational activities, well selected text-books, some refrence books and other historical books.

(b) History Department Library

Subject to the availability of resources there should be a separate history library. It may be housed in the history room. The librarian or the person incharge of it should classify the books properly so that students do not find and difficulty in getting the books issued. History teacher himself should remain in touch with latest books or magazines on the subject and make additions in the library. A number of copies of good books should be purchased. A few copies of prescribed text-books may be purchased for the use of poor students.

13.2 IMPORTANCE AND NEED OF HISTORY LIBRARY

Importance of History Library

Library has a key role in scheme of education. Class-room teaching must be supplemented with the dissemination of knowledge through library. Different types of books in history library can be quite helpful to the students in completing the work assigned to them and to tackle all types of problems emerging from different topics prescribed in their syllabus.

Class-room teaching many a times leaves many gaps and doubts. They can be removed if students work use of good books available in the library. History teacher can help the students in the selection of good books in the library.

A history library, is not only a source of learning and inspiration for students but also serves the need of the teachers. A teacher must keep his knowledge ever fresh and up-to-date, this is possible by making a free use of mathematics library. He can also learn latest methods of teaching history from the new books available in the library. Thus a good history library helps to keep the lamp of historical knowledge burning so as to kindle light in the minds of the students as also the teachers.

Need for Separate History Library

The general library help in encouraging the students to make use of library services, but the students cannot get proper guidance for removing their deficiencies in a particular subject. For this a separate library of subject concerned is essential. A separate library for history is a great necessity for rendering proper help to needy students. Such a library can be housed in history room and can be put under the charge of history teacher. There should be a period of library reading in the time-table so as to enable the students of every class to make use of library. A separate history is essential because of the following reasons:

(i) It helps to bring efficiency in organization of library service.

(ii) History teacher remains in constant touch with the latest books in history.

(iii) It provides a sense of separate identity to history and helps to inculcate interest in the subject.

(iv) The students get better library facilities .

(v) It helps the activities of history club.

(vi) It can be of a help to gifted and bright students.

Thus, it is essential that all out efforts be made to establish a separate history library in every school.

13.3 UTILIZING LIBRARY RESOURCES

Library is a resource centre which is extensively used by all members of the school family. It helps the teacher to enrich curriculum and facilitates personal and professional reading. It helps the students to gain meaningful experiences in reading thinking and forming independent judgements. To the community, it provides for recreational and hobby interests. Library can thus justify its position as a basic tool for instructional programme. Because of the above reasons library occupies a unique position in modern school and it cannot be replaced by any other agency.

The important functions of library are:

(i) It provides material for instructions and for reading.

(ii) It stimulates reading for recreation and enjoyment.

(iii) It teaches the technique of using the library effectively.

(iv) It provides the opportunities to students to assume responsibility.

13.4 MATERIALS FOR HISTORY LIBRARY

History library should contain useful audio-visual aids required for teaching of history. The educational pictures, charts, maps, posters about history be displayed on the walls of library room.

In history library there should be a good collection of history books. The history teacher should be responsible for making a wise selection of books for the library. These books should be of the following types:

1. Text-books

A number of good text-books on various periods of Indian History as also history of the world and history of other important countries, must be made available in the library. It is also very important to note that keeping in view in the excavations in different parts of our country and also in other parts of the world and because of rapidly changing human life in the modern age, new and revised editions of standard text-books should continually be purchased for the school library, with a view to supply up-to-date knowledge and information to teachers and students.

2. Reference Materials

These include reference books, encyclopaedias, dictionaries, year books, biographies, atlases, bibliographies, directories, old manuscripts, old coins and other excavated material, Govt. Gazetteers and the like.

3. Literary Materials

These include biographies autobiographies, fiction, folklore, short-stories, travel books, books of adventure, herostories, romance, drama and poetry. This type of material provides reading for enjoyment and pleasure.

4. Source Materials

These include source books, manuscripts, original accounts of travellers and contemporary historian diaries, proclamations, original letters and dispatches of kings governors and viceroys, treaties, old monuments, historical buildings, sites, old tools, weapons, armours, coins etc.

In addition to the book resources (stated earliar) a good history library be supplemented by periodical, pamphlets, newspapers, magazines etc. This material can be easily and inexpensively used as teaching aid in the teaching of history.

Collateral Reading and the Library

Collateral and supplementary reading is an essential part of history programme. In this subject must collect a lot of information about various facts and movements after consulting many books and periodicals, besides their text-books for solving problems, doing assignments and participating is discussions etc. For this purpose library resources can furnish a rich supply of books, periodicals and pamphlets for collatéral reading. Text-book material must be supplemented by additional reference reading. It is, therefore, that students should be encouraged to read widely on topics of their own interest, both for the sake of information and entertainment. For this purpose they should be guided how to select, read and make use to the knowledge thus obtained. In this way they will be able to form good reading habits along with power study procedures. Students should be encouraged to take notes and to keep a regular record of their reading.

13.5 HOW TO MOTIVATE PUPILS TO UTILIZE LIBRARY RESOURCES

In the beginning of the year, minimum amount of supplementary reading should be fixed by the teacher for each pupil. It may be different for different classes, according to their standard. Even in the case of bright students and poor readers, lists of different types of books, both fiction and non-fiction particularly related with history, should be prepared by the teacher in consultation with the librarian. These lists should be provided to all pupils and they may be asked to read the required number of books, out of which no more than half may be fiction.

To motivate pupils to read, the teacher should set apart some marks in his subject for supplementary reading of this type. They may be added to the total number of marks, the child receives in history at the end of the session. In this way the pupils will definitely be motivated to read.

Moreover, at the time of periodical or monthly tests, at least one compulsory question out of supplementary readers with adequate choice for different categories of pupils, should be given in the question paper. Such a programme should, however, be made known to pupils before hand.

Further, the teacher while teaching a certain unit about a particular period in history should bring with him such books as contain interesting accounts of living conditions prevailing in those periods and read out a few paragraphs in the class from those books. He should, also give to his pupils the names of the books, the names of the authors and those of their publishers and ask them to collect material therefrom, connected with the unit, under study. After a day or two he may ask a pupils who has gone through a certain book and prepared reports and notes, to stand up and read out what he has collected, pertaining to the lesson in hand. In this way, pupils can be motivated to read library books.

Pupils may be asked to collect form different writers, the different views upon a single topic. This is very important because in stead of relying upon only one source, the pupils are encouraged to draw upon several sources of information. This is perhaps the most valuable lesson that can be learned in the library.

Teacher's Duty in the Motivation Programme

The teacher will be able to motivate his pupils for extra reading, if he himself is a wide reader and is familiar with all the books published in his field. He should see that all those books are made available to students from the school library. In addition to books, he should also be a regular reader of newspapers and periodicals. The present day emphasis on current events in the teaching of history demands a good selection of news papers and magazines for the school library. Pupils can only of encouraged to make use of this material if the teacher has himself formed a habit of reading a daily newspaper and at least one or two magazines, related to history and making current-events a basis of study of some important unit in history.

Teacher should also keep a record of the library study of each student as it may help him in evaluating a students performance.

REVISION QUESTIONS

1. What are the important functions of a library?
2. What is the importance and need of a history library ?
3. What are the different library resources for teaching history?
4. How can a history teacher encourage his students to read?

Chapter 14

Role of Text-books in Teaching of History

14.1 INTRODUCTION

We are well aware of the importance and the place of text-books in teaching-learning process. Text-books are the fundamental tools for any teaching-learning process. In past text-books were considered to be the only instrument of importing knowledge and most of the teachers thought that in following a text-books closely, they were doing their duty towards themselves, their pupils etc. It was generally believed that text-books provide the best instructions.

French Revolution played a vital role in the introduction of text-books in education. Leaders of revolution thought that it was very necessary to use text-books for teaching. Later on, the text-books of history were written and prepared on behalf of the State. They were intended to inculcate in the citizens loyalty for the leaders of the revolution and faith in the ideals of the revolution besides making the students to memorize historical events.

Later on, America adopted this method. Books were written there with the objective of inculcating faith and allegiance in the ideals of the American War of Independence. Since then with the growth in education, text-books have come to occupy an important place in the teaching.

14.2 PLACE OF TEXT-BOOKS IN THE TEACHING OF HISTORY

About the importance and the place of text-books in the teaching of history. Some scholars have opined that as far as possible, text-books should not be used in the teaching of history. Some educationists are of the view that teaching should be conducted through the medium of text-books. Johnson says, "The most important aid in the teaching of history is the text-book. It is indeed more than an aid." Both these views are at extremes. Actually, it is a 'golden means' that should be resorted to. Thus, we can say that text-books should be used that but sparingly and economically. They should be used for strengthening the experiences of the students. They should not be taught like reading books or supplementary books in the classroom. These books should be with the students and they should be asked to use them at home for revising the lesson that they have been taught in the class. They may also be encouraged to take help from these text-books for preparing the answers to various questions of home task.

Main utility of text-books lies in the fact that they develop self-confidence in the students and help them to learn to work in a systematic and scientific manner. In addition providing them historical data, they also help the students to learn and draw charts and tables.

It is also suggested that a history text-book should be used in a way that it promotes historical thinking among the pupils. It should also help them in realizing the specific aims and objective set forth in a particular lesson.

Thus, we conclude by saying that "whatever method or methods may be used, the overall effect in the use of text-book should be to achieve the objectives of the teaching of history. This should stimulate the pupils historical imagination to know more of history and to rationalize casual relationship, relating to different historical events. The use of history text-books must be followed by a series of well-graded and thought-provoking questions which make the text-books not an end in itself but a means to realize desirable objective. History text-books, when used effectively, not only vitalize instruction in the class but also give a new meaning to history teaching and learning.[1]

Types of History Text-books

Johnson, in his boom " The Teaching of History in Elementary and Secondary School," has given the following categories of history text-books.

1. "Teaching History in Secondary Schools"-N.C.E.R.T., p. 89.

(a) Precise Text-books. Precise text-books are those which are of a brief and short nature. They present only a skeleton or frame-work of the facts of history. They are not written in a detailed form.

(b) Manuals. Manuals are those text-books which are written in a detailed form. They present a detailed account of the facts and the data. They are just the opposite of the precise text-books, although they leave some room for further development.

(c) Cours. Cours are those text-books which present the subject-matter in complete details of the facts and the data. There is no likelihood for further development. In these text-books, each topic is treated so well that it is quite intelligible without further description.

14.3 QUALITIES AND CHARACTERISTICS OF A GOOD TEXT-BOOK ON HISTORY

All the above mentioned types of history text-books, must have the following essentialities:

1. Diction of the Test-book should be According to the Age and Standard of Pupils

Good text-books on history must be suited to the age, ability and interests of the pupils for whom these are written. Thus they should be child centred and should reflect the stage the child has reached.

2. Text-books should be Course and not Manuals

The two terms *course* and *manuals* are explained below:

Manuals. These are the text-books which are written in a detailed form and they present a detailed account of the facts and the data.

Course. These are the text-books which provide a complete description of the facts and details. There is no likelyhood or their further development/improvement.

3. Text-books should Give a Cause-effect Relationship

Good text-books in history should reveal to the pupils where they are in time, space and society. They should make clear to the pupils the relationship which links the present with the past, the local with the distant and personal and national life with the life and cultures of the people living in the other lands.

4. Text-books should be Well Illustrated

They should contain pictures, maps, charts, time-lines, graphs and sketches of various historical events to make the subject-matter easily understandable and to sustain the interest of the pupils.

5. Text-books should be Written in Clear and Simple Language

The author should write the books in a clear and simple language. It is possible for the author to present the events and thoughts in very clear manner if he has command over the subject. The style adopted in a text-books should be lucid.

6. Free form Bias

A text-books in history should be free from bias and should tell the truth, the whole truth and nothing but the truth.

7. Good Printing and Get-up

The printing and the get-up of the history text-books should be good, otherwise the students shall not get interested in the text-books.

8. Able to Inculcate the Spirit of Internationalism and World Fraternity

History text-books should aim at inculcating, in the students, the feeling of internationalism and world fraternity besides national integration. History text-books should not develop narrow outlook in the students.

9. Element of Selectivity

While construction curriculum, the principle of selectivity is to be kept in mind. Only such events and facts are selected for inclusion in the curriculum that are helpful for upholding social values and make progressive step. This principle should be kept in mind while writing text-books of history. Such events should be emphasised in the history text-books that have influenced mankind and are likely to cast greater influence in the present social set-up.

10. Psychological and Scientific

Text-books of history should be written on the basis of the principles of psychology. They should be scientifically planned and written.

11. List of Contents and Bibliography

There should be a list of contents in the beginning of the book and in the end, there should be a bibliography. List of contents helps the students in finding out the topics which they want to study without wasting much of their time. Bibliography gives them the subject matter for further study of the subject.

12. Reasonably Priced and Within the Reach of Common People

Text-books should be reasonably priced. They should be priced such that it may be possible for the common man to purchase them.

13. Questions at the End

At the end of every chapter, there should be certain questions. These questions should be so designed that they may help the students to recapitulate the topic that they have read. These questions should be psychologically planned and scientifically put.

14.4 ADVANTAGES OF A GOOD TEXT-BOOK

1. It Meets the Needs of Students

A good text-book is written from students' point of view recognising their difficulties and limitations. It, therefore, meets their needs by the use of simple headings, sub-headings, questions, exercises, maps, charts, pictures and other illustrative aids.

2. It Helps in Developing Study Skills

A good text-book gives a common basis on which the process of reading, analysing, outlining and summarising can be mastered.

3. It Gives an Accurate Account of the Subject

A good text-book gives a reasonably correct account of the subject, field or area in an organised manner. Its treatment of the subject-matter is logical and systematic because it is written according to the latest syllabus, prescribed for the class. It, thus, sets a standard of the minimum essential, to be achieved by students of all categories in the class.

4. It Suggests Application of the Material Read

A good text-book in addition to giving the required subject-matter, suggests application of that material through assignments, drills, questions, projects, problems and other exercises of all sorts—reproductive imaginative, dramatic and manual.

5. It Reflects and Establishes Standards

A good text-book indicates what a teacher is to do to teach and what a pupil is to do to learn. Thus, by its teaching aids, it greatly effects methods as well as reflects and establishes the standards of scholarship.

6. It Expands and Limits its Scope and Size According to Needs

A good text-book can expand and delimit its scope, size and content according to the changing requirements of education. Thus, it may sometimes lead and sometimes follow the educational process.

7. It can Serve as Basis for Almost all the Methods

Almost all the methods of teaching can be used with the text-book as a basis of study. Thus, Assignment Procedure of Discussion, Problem, Project and Unit methods can all be used with advantage with the help of the text-book. All these methods and activities are rather suggested in the text-book at the end of each chapter.

8. It can Serve as an Organ of National Integration

By co-ordinating various activities in history a text-book can serve as an organ of national integration. Everyone connected or concerned with national co-ordination in India, has emphasised the improvement of inter-cultural friendship in India by giving a careful consideration to school text-book.

9. It Makes Self-teaching Possible

Imparting of education through lecturing has high value, no doubt. But the impact of even the best spoken words is transitory in character. And in course of time, almost everything listened, goes out of mind. From a text-book, the student can have a connected view of the whole topic as discussed in the class even if he has missed a few lectures.

REVISION QUESTIONS

1. What is the place and importance of text-book in the teaching of history ?
2. It is sometimes argued that good teaching is impossible if the pupil confines himself or herself to a single text-book. How far do you agree to this statement and why ?
3. What are the essential qualities of a good text-book of history ?
4. Discuss the good ways of using a text-book effectively.
5. What are the advantages of using a good text-books ?
6. Discuss the different types of history text-book ? Which of these types would you recommend for use by your students and why?

Chapter 15

Evaluation in History

15.1 INTRODUCTION

Once the teacher has a clear idea of what he will teach and how he will teach it, he is concerned with knowing to what extent children learn from his lesson. This chapter will specifically deal with evaluation of history teaching-learning.

Evaluation is a continuous process which is an integral part of teaching. It is not merely a test at the end of history lesson or unit. Instead evaluation goes an constantly during lesson and units and is clearly related to the teacher's goal and points of view on history teaching. The main aim of any teaching-learning programme is to bring about certain desirable change in pupils.

It is with this definite aim that teaching-learning experiences are designed and planned before hand. *As learning takes place, teachers have to ascertain very frequently the growth and change, taking place in pupils as a result of teaching learning experiences. This is evaluation. To evaluate means to characterise the work or value of something. It is a method of determining the extent to which previously established goals or objectives have been achieved.* It is a "process of making an overlay of the outcomes of an educative experiences against the background of anticipated or stated objectives".

To make improvements in any educational programme we need its evaluation. Good evaluation can only be made in relation to the goals of instructions. Thus there is a close relationship between objectives, experiences and evaluation. A good evaluation rests upon : (i) educational objectives, (ii) learning and behaviour changes, and (iii) tools and techniques of evaluation.

This can be represented diagramatically as under

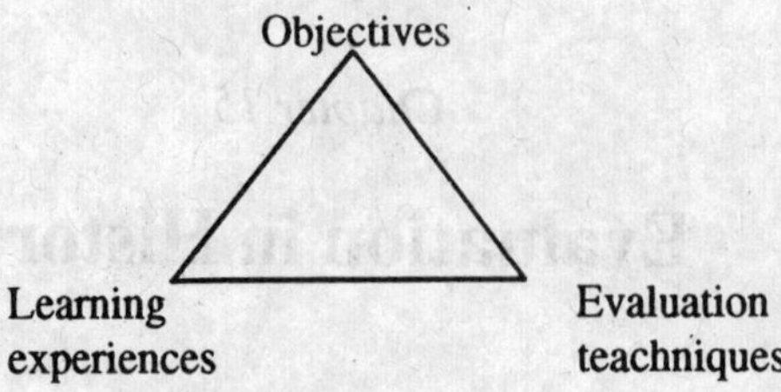

To test efficiency of teaching, to judge the progress of students and to discover their achievements and evaluate the whole system we require some sort of measuring tools. These tools are **tests** or **examinations**. Tests are essential to grade and rank pupils, however, if evaluation is used merely to indicate areas of subject to which students have been exposed or for classifying and categorizing students, a great value is lost. The same loss occurs if evaluation is interpreted only as arriving at numerical or alphabetical ratings for report cards. In this way much of the positive use of evaluation as a means of teaching and learning could be destroyed.

Effective instructional planning and evaluation of students performance have always been stressed on the statement of instructional objectives so that they are of great help to the students. According to Muller, an instructionally usable objective must state the intended outcome in terms of terminal behaviour of students. Terminal behaviour here means the behaviour of the student after class-room instruction and evaluation is possible if the learning outcomes are carefully specified. By combing continuous evaluation with immediate application of what has been learned, the teacher can provide for:

(i) The stimulation of students who learn rapidly to greater growth towards goals be application of advanced works.

(ii) The identification of specific weaknesses and difficulties in functional understanding (concepts, principles, generalizations) and the needed reteaching of varied activities skills or problem solving abilities, and

(iii) The clarification, modification or complete alternation of goals as needed for the unit.

Evaluation, teaching and learning are the three corners of the education system. *Evaluation* is concerned with finding out how far students have learned as a consequence of teaching. There are two kinds or evaluation depending upon whether the comparison of students is made with some absolute performance standard or with other students of group. These are known as *criterion referenced evaluation* and *norm referenced evaluation*.

Norm—Referenced Evaluation

It accesses the students performance relative to other students of the group. Students are awarded marks and relative ranks in this method of evaluation.

Criterion—Referenced Evaluation

It assesses the students performance in terms of a specified performance standard or criterion without any mention of the performance levels of the other students of the group. This evaluation method is related to mastery and developmental test.

15.2 PURPOSE OF EVALUATION

The main purpose of evaluation is:

(i) for determining the teaching-learning process,

(ii) for revision of the curriculum,

(iii) to provide an objective basis for reporting progress of students,

(iv) for securing effective co-operation from the parents and the community,

(v) for determining the policies of promotion, and

(vi) to provide suitable guidance to pupils, on the basis of their evaluation.

Thus we find that evaluation is an essential part of the educational process. It helps in realising the goals of instructions. It points out the defects in teaching-learning process. It also helps in ascertaining the effectiveness of the curriculum, methods and devices of teaching etc.

15.3 SPECIFIC OBJECTIVES OF EVALUATION IN HISTORY

Following are the specific objectives of evaluation in history:

I. Measurement of Factual Knowledge

The evaluation is done to determine the extent and rate of pupils growth along the line of aims and objectives of teaching of history. It is expected that each individual pupil will acquire some definite, knowledge, information and concepts. Such a knowledge helps in creating a fellow-feeling and also helps to develop clear thinking and critical judgement. Thus, it becomes essential to measure achievements in this direction.

II. Diagnosing Weaknesses

Evaluation in history is essential to discover specific weaknesses of the student. Making use of this information teacher can take remedial measures for removal to the weakness.

III. For Predicting Future Achievements

Evaluation helps in determining the potential achievements of pupils. It also helps to discover their special abilities and attitudes. It thus helps to predict the future success of the student and to provide him guidance for future educational opportunities, vocational students etc.

IV. Stimulate Instructions

Evaluation stimulates both teacher and the pupil to work harder so as to attain a higher level.

Evaluation gives us enough information that can be used to meet the criticism of parents. It also helps the teacher in directing the intellect and emotions of his pupil in such a way that they become useful citizen of the society.

15.4 CHARACTERISTICS OF GOOD TEST IN HISTORY

A good test in history should have the following characteristics:

1. Validity

The test should be valid. It should fulfil the objectives for which it is meant. For this it should be free from defects that are likely to affect the valid results.

2. Reliability

Any test can be considered reliable if it gives some results every time when it is used for testing the individual's ability under same conditions. An objective test is bound to be reliable.

The reliability of a test is affected by the following factors, thus to be reliable it should be free from

(a) The whims of the examiner.

(b) The physical and mental condition of the student.

(c) The language of questions—lack of clearness or any ambiguities is statements.

(d) Lack of clear-cut instructions for marking.

(e) Inefficient method of scoring.

A reliable test is not influenced by subjective conditions, it is objective.

3. Comprehensiveness

Any good test should be comprehensive, i.e., it should assess knowledge, skills, abilities, attitudes etc., as adequately as possible. No aspect of the curriculum should be ignored while making evaluation.

4. Administratibility

It should be easy to administer, economical in time and money, easy to score and interpret. The direction of the test should be clear-cut. There should be answer keys for scoring.

5. Capable of Maintaining the Interest of the Student

Any good test should be able to capture the interest of the students and maintain it. Thus it should be interesting for the students. A good test is motivating for the students and stimulates their best effects. It should be neither too easy nor too difficult. It should never be used as a means of punishment.

6. Diagnosticity

A good test is diagnostic. The aim of diagnosis is to analyse the difficulties of a student in a particular phase of work. The aim is to reveal reliable information concerning his weaknesses so as to overcome them by concerted action and remedial teaching. In this way it would help the teacher to guide them properly and adopt remedial measures to eliminate their weak points.

7. Utility

A good test is useful in various ways. For example a test result may be used for improvement of teaching, may be useful to measure some desired quality/ability in the student, useful in finding out deficiencies in pupils so that the remedial measures may be taken up for their removal.

15.5 TYPES OF TESTS OR EXAMINATIONS

Examination means *to test the knowledge of a subject*. It is a method of testing the knowledge of the students. The present system of examinations in over country came into in the 19th century with the introduction of English language.

Generally, the tests are of two types:

(i) Traditional or Essay type examination.

(ii) New type test or examination.

15.6 EVALUATION AND THE TRADITIONAL TYPE OF EXAMINATION

The traditional type examination was mainly based on essay. It measured only the factual knowledge retained by the pupils. Memorization and cramming were the chief criteria for promotion to next higher class. It was, thus, a "one way street" which deprived children of varied abilities, a chance of continuing their studies in the school. Attitudes, emotions, interests and appreciations had no place in the examination programme.

The new idea of evaluation is more comprehensive which includes the testing of both tangible and intangible qualities. It is related to total learning situation. It is a meaningful process, utilizing many sources as they apply to the objectives of a democratic and forward-looking educational structure. It takes in to account the growth of the child as a whole individual and in his total environment. In evaluation one has to know where the pupils were at the beginning of the teaching learning process, get a record of changes brought in them and judge how good those changes are in relation to established objectives. Evaluation, therefore, includes many facets. It is both objective and subjective. It comes both from within and without. Evaluation is thus, a continuous and developing process which must form an essential part of educational programme. It must be made part of each problem and each unit of work in history and should relate to the objectives of that unit or problem.

Defects of Traditional Type of Tests or Examinations

Some of the defects from which traditional type of examination suffer are:

A. Defects from the Point of View of Students

(i) Essay type tests are less objective and so they lack **Validity**. This type of tests can reveal child's cramming capacity only.

(ii) *These tests lack reliability.* A student is compelled to have a selective reading. He depends more on guess papers and so there is an element of chance.

(iii) It keeps the students busy and full of nervous tension. The study does not spread over the whole year and is limited to a short period just before the examinations. Thus a habit of irregular study is developed in the student.

B. Defects of Essay Type Examination from the Point of View of the Teacher

(i) The teacher covers only a limited and important portion of course because his aim is to see that maximum number of his students pass the examinations.

(ii) The teaching programme of the teacher is wholly examination oriented and the basic principle of teaching his students are given least consideration.

(iii) The teacher is compelled to encourage his students to cramming which is not a psychological method of teaching.

(iv) Since a teacher is judged by the results of his students so every thing becomes subservient to the examinations.

(v) To show good results sometimes the teacher devotes a good deal of his time to indulge in guess work which affects his teaching.

C. Defects from the Point of View of Achievements

(i) Essay type tests are not comprehensive and some students may get good marks only because the questions have been set from the portion prepared by them.

(ii) These tests are not objective and the score of a student depends upon various factors such as examiner's mood and whims etc.

(iii) This type of tests are not useful from the point of view of improvement. They fail to throw light on the defects of teaching-learning processes or the defects of the curriculum.

From the above are can conclude that essay type examination is not correct method of evaluation in history. The improvement in system of evaluation is possible if following suggestions are given due consideration.

(a) **Improvement in Essay Type Questions**. The language of the questions should be clear and precise and clear cut directions be given for scoring. Shorter questions spread over the whole course be set.

(b) **Use of Objective Tests**. In addition to essay type tests, some objective type tests be used for evaluation. The objective tests can be of the following type:

(i) True-false type

(ii) Completion type

(iii) Multiple choice type

(iv) Matching type

(v) Short answer type

(c) **Use of Oral Tests**. In such oral tests questions are asked and the students answer them orally. Such questions require quick recall and thinking. These tests helps in assessing the ability of the students to apply the knowledge of facts in different situations.

(d) **Assessment of Regular Work**. For such assessment a record of child's developments should be kept. Such a record may be kept for his home-work, practical work etc., and this should be taken into consideration while assessing a student.

Thus, we find that no single device in enough and a judicious blend of various evaluation tools is the best approach.

15.7 EVALUATING THE RESULTS OF HISTORY INSTRUCTIONS

A complete evaluation programme in history should include the following instructions:

1. For evaluating knowledge information and concepts:

(i) Oral tests, (ii) Essay-type tests, (iii) Objective-type tests, (iv) Testing the pupil's day-to-day work, in the class.

2. *For evaluating skills i.e.,* assessment of the process of work, of actual performance and of furnished product etc.

3. For evaluating attitudes, interests and values:

(i) Observation, *(ii)* Conferences and interviews, *(iii)* Anecdotal Records, *(iv)* Diaries and Logs, *(v)* Work Samples, *(vi)* Pupils' Interest Inventories, *(vii)* Sociometry, *(viii)* Objective Standardized Tests, and *(ix)* Cumulative Records.

For evaluation of knowledge, information and concepts. We carry out the: *(i)* Oral Tests, *(ii)* The essay type tests, and *(iii)* Objective type tests.

The oral tests and the essay type tests have already been dealt in previous section and here we take up the discussion of objective type tests.

The objective type tests in common use are:

(i) The standardized tests.

(ii) The non-standardized or teacher made tests.

The standardized tests are the work of experts who have established their validity and reliability, fixed definite and uniform procedures for using them and providing keys for scoring. A test is said to be standardized if the conditions under which it has to be given are standardized to ensure uniformity of procedure.

The standardized tests are of four types:

(*i*) Achievement tests.

(*ii*) Diagnostic tests.

(*iii*) Intelligence tests.

(*iv*) Aptitude and personality tests.

Diagnostic and Achievement Tests

The aim of diagnosis is to analyse the difficulties of students in a particular phase of work. The aim is to reveal reliable information concerning his weaknesses in order to overcome them by concerted action and for remedial teaching. It can also be used as an inventory test to find out how much the student knows about a given phase of the subject-matter. Diagnostic tests are used to discover and analyse pupils difficulties with a view to setting up specific remedial measures to correct errors and remove difficulties.

A diagnostic test is different from achievement test in that the main purpose of a diagnostic test is to study the nature of difficulties expe-ienced by pupils. While constructing a diagnostic test. The teacher has to consider the individual difficulties experienced by students in solving problems. The test items should also give due consideration to the varying abilities of pupils in solving different types of problems. The age norm, the grade norm etc., should also be given due consideration. Before constructing such a test a pilot study be conducted over a given area or unit and its results statistically analysed before finalising the test.

The reliability coefficient of the test has to be calculated and then the diagnostic test can be deemed to be fit for administration over a large sample.

Appropriate remedial instructions be given and for this careful planning is essential. The causes of failure on solving a problem are to be hypothesized systematically.

The importance of diagnostic tests is due to the following:

(*i*) Nature of the subject matter.

(*ii*) Difficulties experienced by students as a group.

(*iii*) Difficulties experienced by certain individual.

An **achievement test** is used to measure the degree of mastery of skills, fundamental concepts, processes and general knowledge of the subject, attained by the student. The achievement test is valid when it can measure the extent to which the purpose for which it has been constructed.

Importance of Blue-print in Constructing Achievement Test

The **blue-print** there means the plan that the teacher has in evaluating the performance of the pupils.

The blue-print concerns itself to the knowledge acquired by means of study, remembering, thinking, solving problems, formulating hypothesis. It is here that the formulation of instructional objectives and their respective behavioural changes can be clearly identified.

In a **blue-print** the objectives are listed horizontally. They are knowledge, understanding, application and skill. Again horizontally forms of test items are indicated. They are essay questions, short answer questions and objective questions.

Vertically we find the subject divided into sub-units. The question paper should cover all the sub-units and all the objective. The score for each type of questions viz. essay, short answer and objective type should be fixed.

It is desirable that most of the final examinations in schools should be achievement tests.

1. Aptitude and Personality Test

These tests are intended to measure the trait of temperament and character. These are in the form of inventories and rating scales. They are more qualitative than quantitative.

2. Non-standardised Tests

They are informal type new tests. They are generally of two main types (a) **recognition,** and (b) **recall**.

(a) Recognition type questions include true/false, matching, multiple choice etc.

(b) Recall questions include, i.e., completion type or short answer questions.

This type of objective tests have the following merits:

(i) They have little or no scope of subjectivity.

(ii) They are more reliable.

(iii) These are comprehensive.

(iv) There is no chance element in them.

(v) They are easy to administer and easy to score

(vi) They are economical in respect to time.

However, they also suffer from certain drawbacks. Some of these are as follows:

(i) They fail to test the organising ability of the child.

(ii) They fail to develop thinking and reasoning power of the students.

(iii) They put more emphasis on factual knowledge and very little importance is given to processes, methods, originality of thought etc.

(iv) They encourage guess work.

(v) These tests are not diagnostic.

(vi) These tests may pose some administrative difficulties as there may be indiscipline in the students. They may use unfair means, whisper answers or make same gestures.

(vii) It needs a lot of time and labour to prepare such a test.

Different Types of Objective Tests

We now take up the discussion of various types of objective tests.

1. Completion Type of Test or Memory Recall. This type of test consists of questions that are either sentences or statements, in between the words a blank is left within the body of the material. Sometimes the space is left in the margin which has to be filled in by the students. Given below are a few examples of this type of test:

(i) The official language of the Mughals was—-.

(ii) The Third Battle of Panipat was fought between —- and —-.

(iii) The headquarters of U.N.O are at —-.

(iv) The Britishers first came to India as traders. They formed the

East India Company in—-. Their trade rivals in India were —-.

In this type of tests words used are quite important and so the statement or the question should be worded carefully leaving no scope for ambiguity. If the student get confused the very purpose of such a test is lost.

(2) True and False Type. In this type, a number of statements are given. Some of these are true and some are false. The students are required to tick ✓ or write 'yes' before a correct statement.

Examples

(i) Guru Nanak was the founder of Bhakti Movement. Yes/No.

(ii) Agriculture was the major occupation of people in the primitive age. Yes/No.

(iii) Aurungzeb was a tolerant ruler. Yes/No.

(iv) The external policy of Ranjit Singh was the cause of the downfall of Sikh monarchy immediately after his death. Yes/ No.

(v) Razia Begam was a famous Mughal Queen. Yes/No.

These tests can cover a wide range of subject-matter and wide sampling of knowledge is possible. There is an objectivity in scoring. Such a test is not difficult to construct but while constructing such a test the care be taken not to put very descriptive statements before the students.

(3) Multiple Choice Tests. Such tests contain a number of items, each of which has two or three responses. One of the responses in each item is correct. The students are required to tick the correct response.

1. The establishment of Indian National Congress was essential because

(*a*) The hold of the English was getting weaker day by day.

(*b*) The administration was defective.

(*c*) There was national consciousness among the Indian intelligentia.

(*d*) It was organised by foreign element that was against the English rule.

2. Mark out the correct answer

(*a*) First World War was fought in 1930/1857/1914.

(*b*) The Indian National Congress was established in 1702/ 1885/1858.

(*c*) The Third Battle of Panipat was fought in 1625/1526/1761.

(*d*) Mahatma Gandhi was born in 1771/1869/1902.

This type of test requires memory as also the correct knowledge and a good vocabulary.

(4) Matching Type Test. In these tests, in each item, there are two columns. Each item in the first column is to be matched with the relevant item of the second column, not given in the same order. To avoid guess work, the items in the second may be more or less in number than items in the first column.

Examples

Column A	*Column B*
1................The place where the original inhabitants of India lived.	1. Vinobha
2..............The international seat of learning in ancient India.	2. Lambardar
3...............The European explorer whose efforts resulted in the discovery of India.	3. Dictatorship
4...............The person who started the Bhoodan Movement.	4. Indus Vally
5...............Government that is run by one man.	5. Vasco-de-Gama
6...............The highest mountain peak in the world.	6. Nalanda

(5) Time-sequence form. This type of questions contain a list of items and the student is required to arrange them on the basis of chronology.

Examples

(1) Re-arrange the following in correct chronological order:

....................Quit India Movement.

....................Simon Commission.

.....................The First partition of Bengal.

.....................The starting of Non-Co-operation Movement.

.....................Permanent Settlement of Bengal.

.....................The Subsidiary System.

.....................The Battle of Samugarh.

.....................Foundation of Indian National Congress.

Requirements of the New Type of Tests

New type tests have to be carefully constructed. The following precautions be taken otherwise these tests are likely to lose the utility.

Careful Planning and Constructions. For this the following things are needed:

(a) Determination of the Purpose: The basic purpose of the test should be decided first.

(b) Relation of the Test in Accordance with the Purpose: After purpose has been decided, the test has to be found out which would suit the purpose.

(c) Objective Questions. The questions that are constructed should be objective.

(d) Ability of the Student to be Kept in Mind. The individual differences and the mental ability of the students should be kept in mind, otherwise the purpose shall not be served.

(e) Scoring Key to be Prepared. The scoring key that provides answer to the questions must be prepared. Unless it is done, the purpose shall not be served. Without it, it shall be different to award marks.

(f) Standardisations. These tests need standardisation. Then only it is possible to do away with the element of subjectivity.

(g) Intelligent Planning. It is not possible for all the teachers to plan these tests. These tests have to be planned and constructed by intelligent teachers as they require intelligent planning.

While planning these tests following should be avoided :

(i) Difficult words and sentences should be avoided.

(ii) Text-book sentences should be avoided.

(iii) Ambiguities should be avoided.

(iv) Clues and suggestions should be avoided.

REVISION QUESTIONS

1. Define evaluation and state briefly the difference between evaluation and traditional types of examination.
2. State briefly the need and importance of evaluation in the teaching learning process.
3. What is the difference between appraisal and measurement ?
4. State by actual examples how objectives, learning experiences and evaluation are inter-related.
5. What are the important objectives of evaluation in history ? To what extent is the present system of examination based on these objectives?
6. Discuss a complete evaluation programme in history.
7. What are objective-type tests ? Distinguish between standardized and non-standardized objective-type tests.
8. Mention briefly the main advantages and disadvantages of new-type tests.
9. State the important forms of new-type tests with suitable examples in each case.
10. What important points should a teacher bear in mind while constructing new-type tests ?
11. Give two specimens of evaluation test-items on your subject, based on definite objectives and behaviour changes.

Chapter 16

Lesson Planning

16.1 INTRODUCTION

A proper planning of lessons is the key to effective teaching. The teacher must know in advance the subject-matter and mode of its delivery in the class-room. This planning will give the teacher idea of how to introduce the topic, how to develop the key concepts, how to correlate the concepts to real life situations and how to conclude the lesson.

According to Bossing, "Lesson plan is the title given to the statement of the achievements to be realised and the specific means by which these are to be attained as a result of the activities engaged in, during the period".

L.B. Stands conceives a lesson plan as "Plan of action" implemented by the teacher in the class-room.

G.H. Green says, " the teacher who has planned his lesson wisely related to his topic and to his class will be in a position to enter the class-room without any anxiety, ready to embark with confidence upon a job he understands and prepared to carry it to a workmanable conclusion. He has far seen the difficulties that are likely to arise, and prepared himself to deal with them. He knows the aims, his lesson is intended to fulfil, and he has marshelled his own resources for the purpose, and because he is free of anxiety, he will be able cooly to estimate the value of his work as the lesson proceeds, equally aware of failure and success and prepared to learn from both."

Though a syllabus is prescribed for each class yet the teacher is at liberty to draw up his own teaching syllabus. It is best to organise the teaching syllabus around a few broad areas of experience of pupils. For this purpose the syllabus is divided into a number of units.

16.2 UNIT PLANNING

A *unit* is a related learning segment made up of a few lessons along with an outline of its execution in the class-room. Thus a unit will consist of both the subject matter and methodology of its delivery to students.

Hoover defines unit as, " the teaching unit is a group of related concepts from which a given set of instructional and educational experiences is desired. Unit normally range for these to six weeks long".

In view of Preston, a unit is a large chunk or a block of related subject-matter as can be overviewed by the learner.

After having divided the syllabus into a number of teaching units the teacher will decide the time that could be allocated to each unit. After that he could break up each unit into a number of lessons and each lesson should be complete in itself. After that the teacher will enter in his diary the scheme of work under the headings (see table).

TABLE

Unit no......

Date	*Course Content*	*Demonstration*	*Equipment/ Material*	*Students activities*	*Remarks Reference*

Advantages of Unit Planning

(i) It provides a basic course structure around which specific class activities can be organised.

(ii) It enables the teacher to integrate the basic course concepts and those of related areas into various teaching experiences.

(iii) It provides an opportunity to the teacher to keep a balance between various dimensions of the prescribed course.

(iv) It enables the teacher to break away from traditional text-book teaching.

16.3 LESSON PLANNING

Like planning of other activities. Planning of lesson is also needed. Without proper planning of the lesson, it is not possible for the teacher to carry out the teaching successfully. It has been rightly remarked: "Without planning the teacher is just like a ship moving in the sea without any aim and destination."

Advantages of Lesson Planning

Some of the advantages of lesson planning are as under:

(i) Lesson planning makes the work regular, organised and more systematic.

(ii) It induces confidence in the teacher.

(iii) It makes teacher quite conscious of the aim which makes him conscious of attitudes he wants to develop in his students.

(iv) It saves a lot of time.

(v) It helps in making correlation between the concepts with the pupils environment.

(vi) It stimulates the teacher to ask striking questions.

(vii) It provides more freedom in teaching.

(viii) It makes possible for the teacher to move in a scientific manner.

16.4 FEATURES OF A LESSON PLAN

Some important features of a lesson-plan are as under:

1. Objectives

All the cognitive objective that are intended to be fulfilled should be listed in the lesson-plan. Objectives should be formulated in terms of changes desired in behaviour of students. Objectives, as we know, have two specifications; the content specification and the competence specification. We have to mention clearly what type of changes we are going to bring in different domains cognitive, affective and psychomoter of students behaviour within a particular type of content.

The objective should be written in specific behavioural terms stating exactly what the learner will be doing, or saying when he demonstrates that he has achieved the aims of an instructional sequence. Walbesser constructing behavioural objectives, listed four requirements for the construction of objectives:

1. Words denoting the stimulus situation which initiates the performance should appear in the description of the objective.
2. An action verb which denotes observable behaviour must be contained in the description.
3. A word denoting the object acted upon, must be contained in the description.
4. A phrase which indicates the characteristics of the performance that determines its correctness or acceptability must be included in the description of the objectives.

An example of a well stated behavioural objective in history is:

The students will be able to recall and recognise the facts and events relating to the period of Ashoka.

In selecting the objectives for a particular lesson in history, the teacher, first of all, should see that they are worthwhile learning out-comes, pertinent to the course. Secondly, the teacher should be clear and definite in his mind about the desired learning outcomes. Lastly, the objective should be feasible. In other words, it should be attained by the procedure followed and within the time allotted for it.

2. Content

The subject-matter that is intended to be covered should be limited to the prescribed time. The matter must be interesting and it should be related to pupils previous knowledge. It should be related to daily life situations.

3. Methods

The most appropriate method be chosen by the teacher. The method chosen should be suitable to the subject-matter to be taught. Suitable teaching aids must also be identified by the teacher. Teacher may also use supplementary aids to make his lesson more effective.

4. Evaluation

Teacher must evaluate his lesson to find the extent to which he has achieved the aim of his lesson. Evaluation can be done even by recapitulation of subject-matter through suitable questions.

In writing a lesson plan the following points be written down:

(i) Date,
(ii) Period,
(iii) Class,
(iv) Duration,
(v) Subject,
(vi) Topic,
(vii) General objectives,
(viii) Specific objectives,
(ix) Previous knowledge of the students,
(x) Teaching aids and materials to be used,
(xi) Introduction,
(xii) Statement of object,
(xiii) Presentation,
(xiv) Generalisations,
(xv) Recapitulations,
(xvi) Black-board summary,
(xvii) Hand-work.

16.5 STEPS IN LESSON PLANNING (HERBARTION STEPS)

Formal Steps in lesson planning are discribed as follows:

(i) Introduction

It pertains to preparing and motivating children to the lesson content by linking it to the previous knowledge of the students, by arousing curiosity of the children and by making an appeal to their senses. This prepares the child's mind to receive new knowledge. This steps though so important must be brief. It may involve testing of pervious knowledge of the child. Sometimes the curiosity of the pupil can be aroused by some chart, model, story or even by some useful discussion. It serves as the bridge between what the students know and what they are going to learn.

(ii) Statement of Aim

After the introduction which is necessarily based on students previous knowledge, the teacher states the aim of the lesson he is going to teach. It should be stated in clear and precise terms so that it brings home to the pupils the importance of the lesson.

(iii) Presentation

It involves the stating of the object of lesson and exposure of students to new information. The actual lesson begins and both teacher and students participate. Teacher should make use of different teaching aids to make his lesson effective. Teacher should draw as much as is possible from students making use of judicious questions. In selecting the method the teacher should keep in mind the age and competence of the pupils. Story-telling method may be used in primary and upper primary classes, source method in secondary and higher secondary classes.

(iv) Association

It is always desirable that new ideas or knowledge be associated to the daily life situations by citing suitable examples and by drawing comparison with the related concepts. This steps is all the more important when we are establishing principle or generalising definitions.

(v) Generalisation

In this step teacher makes an effort so that the students draw the conclusion themselves.

(vi) Application and Recapitulation

Recapitulation means asking the pupils to reproduce what they have learnt. As we have already stated, recapitulation at the end of the lesson, also serves the purpose of application. Recapitulation is looking back and surveying briefly the path that has been just covered or travelled. It is connecting up all the essential parts of the lesson, in an orderly and systematic way in a few minutes. Recapitulation will not be possible unless and until the pupils have thoroughly understood the lesson in all its essential parts and details. Thus, recapitulation is a very valuable mental exercise which makes studies more efficient and gives increased mastery of the subject-matter.

Above steps are only guide lines and in many lessons it is not possible to follow all these steps.

There is another way of lesson planning that is gaining currency these days. It is known as *Glover Plan*. This plan has four steps as follows:

(i) Questioning. Teacher must introduce and develop his lesson through related and sequential questions. Start the lesson by asking questions about previous knowledge of the students. The questions should then lead to new knowledge under consideration.

Lesson can also be introduced with the help of some teaching aid like picture, chart, or model etc. The introduction can also be made by describing a situations or by telling a short story.

However, teacher should bear in mind that introduction in brief and interesting.

(ii) Discussion. For discussion the class be divided into smaller groups and in such groups students be encouraged to express their ideas and opinions freely this helps the students in removal of their difficulties.

(iii) Investigation. The students are encouraged to do a project or investigation on the lesson topic either individually or in small groups by processing information.

(iv) Expression. It concerns the strategy in which the students and teachers communication of ideas through observation and listening (passive expression) or through doing (active expression) or by arranging learning situations (organisational expression).

In developing a lesson a teacher must keep in mind the following psychological principles:

(i) Principle of Section and Division. The teacher should wisely select and divide the learning material into smaller segments. It is also for the teacher to decide about the questions of subject- matter to be covered by him and that which has to be illicited from the students.

(ii) Principle of Successive Clarity. It is for the teacher to see that the different learning segments of lesson are well structured, sequenced and connected. Teacher must ensure, at each segment, that students leave grasped the subject-matter given to them.

(iii) Principle of Integration. Teacher should conclude his lesson only after combining various learning segments to produce some generalisations.

Design for Writing a Lesson Plan

The style given below is adopted for writing a lesson plan

Class: Date:

Subject: Duration:

Topic:

Instructional Material: --

General objectives: --

Specific objectives: --

Previous knowledge: --------------------------------------

Questions: ------------------------------------

1. --------------------------- ?

2. --------------------------- ?

3. ---------------------------- ?

Introduction: ------------------------------------

Questions:

1. ---------------------------- ?

2. ---------------------------- ?

Announcement of Aim: --

Presentation:

Matter	*Method*	*B.B. Summary*

Conclusions: --

Applications: --

Recapitulations: ------------------------------------

1. -- ?

2. -- ?

Home Task: ------------------------------------

16.6 SOME MODEL LESSON PLANS

Lesson Plan-1

Class: VI　　　　Time: 40 minutes

Date: Nov. 6, 1994　　　　Period: IV

Subject: Indian History

Topic: Life of Shivaji

General Aims

(i) To inculcate in pupils a sense of patriotism by acquainting them with the great deeds and lives of great men of their country.

(ii) To develop in the students the qualities of chivalry and bravery and to encourage them to become great.

(iii) To develop in students the curiosity to know more and more about history.

(iv) To develop in students the right attitudes of fellow feeling, friendliness, co-operation, toleration and international understanding.

Specific Aims

(i) To make students familiar with the life and administration of Shivaji.

(ii) To develop in the students, the spirit of patriotism and love for motherland in the students.

Teaching Aids

(i) A full size picture of Shivaji

(ii) A map of India (political) showing the boundaries of the territory under the rule of Shivaji.

Previous Knowledge

Students are already familiar with the names of Lord Rama, Lord Krishna, Ashoka the great etc.

Introduction

The lesson will be introduced by asking the following questions:

(i) Name a few historical personalities born in India.

Ans. Rama, Krishan, Ashoka etc.

(ii) Name the Marahatta personality who struggled hard for keeping India free from English domination.

Not getting a proper reply, the teacher will announce the name of Shivaji and will also announce the topic for the day.

Presentation

Matter	*Method*	*B.B Summary*
Shivaji was Marahatta Chieftain. He was born in 1927 A.D. Guru Ram Das was taking active part to write the Marahattas who were willing to lay down their lives for their religion and motherland. Their slogan was, "Destroy the enemy of motherland."	When was Shiviji born?	1627 A.D.
Shavaji was the sun of Shahji who was a courtier of Suttan of Ahmadnagar. Because of extremely busy life of his father Shivaji was brought up by his mother Jija Bai. She told the stories of Ramayana, Mahabharta, etc.These stories made Shivaji a great patriot. He was full of ambitions to defend his motherland.	Who was the father of Shivaji? What was the name of Shivaji's mother? Which stories were narrated to Shivaji by his mother? What effect these stories have on Shivaji?	Shahji. Jija Bai. Ramayana, Mahabharta etc. They made him a great patriot.

Recapitulation

The teacher will ask the following questions:

1. When was Shivaji born ?
2. What was Shivaji's father ?
3. What was the main aim of Marahattas at that time ?

Home Work

Write down an outline of the life of Shivaji.

Chapter 17

Miscellaneous

17.1 INTRODUCTION

In this chapter some topic which occupy an important place in teaching of history are taken up. Some of these topic have been dealt with in some other chapters of the book and may be repeated here in a detailed manner. However, an effort has been made to make any such repetitions.

17.2 ROLE OF DRAMATISATION IN TEACHING OF HISTORY

Dramatisation is a device that helps the history teacher to make the past real phenomena. History deals not only with places and objects but also with events, ideas, and institutions which have been preserved through verbal symbols. Moreover, it does not proceed through isolated phenomenon but it has a causal sequences, one event leading to another event and the process continues. Human intentions, designs and motives behind every event cannot be presented through visual symbols. They can be made real only if they are acted upon by human beings.

Dramatisation is an attempt to act or to do as other have acted or done. It is the depiction of characters, movements, and activities of a story or a play through facial expression, gesture and bodily actions accompanied by the use of language. " It attempts to tell the story in more vivid manner than by word alone, and to enrich the appeal of the play through the addition of the pictorial element found in the movement of speaking characters across the stage." With its concrete appeal to the sense of sight as well as to the sense of hearing dramatisation makes and ardent appeal to the children.

In history dramatisation is concerned with reconstruction of past experiences of historical significance. It provides opportunity for vivid realistic and full representation of a happening or a situation in history.

It attempts to transcend the barrier of time and place and relives the experience concerned. Through the use of language, accompanied by bodily actions and supported by proper setting, it helps to bring out the customs, the language, and the mannerisms of the period.

For example, if the life of Shivaji is enacted, the actor who plays the role of Shivaji, enacts not his deeds but those of Shivaji.

Dramatisation is full of education, potentialities. It presents an emotional situation which is necessary for effective learning. It provides an outlet for the discharge of extra energy of the pupils and thereby gives them poise and balance of mind. In addition, dramatisation provides and excellent opportunity for group work and social participation and many practical works in history can be correlated with it.

In dramatisation, the pupils who play the role of different characters of history, have to feel like those characters and to a degree have to become the characters. K.P. Choudhury says, "The pupils assimilate the essential facts by playing the different historical characters and by reconstructing the important historical events, in the connection. Those who do not directly participate in dramatisation but witness it, also get in the spirit and in case of successful acting they are also carried away with the characters—the experience becoming almost as real to them as to the actors." Thus, dramatisation is an effective method of providing an opportunity for learning by doing in history.

Elements of Learning by Doing

Dramatisation is a useful activity. It helps to provide stable knowledge and the students learn by doing and so their experiences are strengthened. Prof. Davy has observed, "When a pupils learns by doing, he is relishing both—mental and physical experiences which have proved important to the human race."

Kinds of Dramatisation

Dramatisation may range for simple attempts of the pupils at acting out of roles to well rehearsed and thoroughly set full length plays. Between these two extremes lies such other forms as pantomines, pageants, tableau, puppet show etc.

(i) **Full Length Play**. It provides an opportunity for the vivid, realistic and full representation of an idea, happening or a situation in History. They can be enacted only after thorough preparation that require careful rehearsals, proper costumes and well arranged setting etc. It is a type of a **prepared dramatisation (formal Dramatization)**.

The history teacher may undertake even less formal dramatization (**Informal dramatisation**). While teaching in the class-room the historical events may be presented to the pupils by asking them to play the role of different historical characters. The application of knowledge gained or recapitulation may also be done with the help of dramatisation.

(ii) **The Pantomine**. Pantomime is a play in which the participants express themselves through bodily actions which are generally accompanied by music. It helps the students to be communicative with facial expressions and bodily gestures. In history we come across a number of situations wherein action without words in by far the most telling mode of communication.

(iii) **The Pageant**. It is another form of dramatization. It helps to depict an idea by arranging a spectacle. The great emperors in India, the great social and religious reformers may appear in a line each with his distinctive dress. Indian art through the ages, the best works from architecture, sculpture and painting may also be presented through pageants.

(iv) **The tableau**. It is even a more effective device for representing emotional theme is tableau. It is a picture-like scene of human characters, presented against the back ground of their action. Against the back ground of misery Budha may be shown as appearing like a light or Ashoka may be shown to be receiving a new inspiration in the battle field of Kalinga.

(v) **Puppetry**. Puppetry is one of the most significant forms of dramatisation. Distinct from human drama its appeal is universal. Its characters have their own personality and are not swayed by human emotions. For the beginners provide a natural charm and leave enough scope for imagination. Puppetry presents ideas with extreme simplicity without elaborate scenery or costume—yet effectively. Themes like India on the Day of Independence, a Session of the Congress, and